Writings in Periodicals
Edited by W.E.B. Du Bois

Selections from
THE HORIZON

THE COMPLETE PUBLISHED WORKS
OF
W.E.B. DU BOIS

HERBERT APTHEKER, EDITOR

Writings in Periodicals
Edited by W.E.B. Du Bois

Selections from
THE HORIZON

COMPILED AND EDITED BY

HERBERT APTHEKER

KRAUS-THOMSON ORGANIZATION LIMITED

White Plains, New York

First printing 1985

Printed in the United States of America

Library of Congress Cataloging in Publication Data

Du Bois, W. E. B. (William Edward Burghardt), 1868-1963.
  Selections from the Horizon.

  (Writings in periodicals edited by W.E.B. Du Bois)
(The Complete published works of W.E.B. Du Bois)
  Includes bibliographical references and index.
  1. Afro-Americans—Addresses, essays, lectures.
2. United States—Race relations—Addresses, essays,
lectures. I. Aptheker, Herbert, 1915-   .
II. Horizon (Washington, D.C.) III. Title. IV. Series:
Du Bois, W. E. B. (William Edward Burghardt), 1868-1963.
Selections. 1983. V. Series: Du Bois, W. E. B.
(William Edward Burghardt), 1868-1963. Works. 1982.
E185.97.D73A25 1985a   305.8'96073   85-5530
ISBN 0-527-25350-2

Contents

Introduction

An important feature of W.E.B. Du Bois's lifelong struggle against racism and for democracy was his editorship of magazines. All of Du Bois's magazines—the *Moon* (1905–1907), *The Horizon: A Journal of the Color Line* (1907–1910), *The Crisis* (1910–1934), the *Brownies' Book* (for children, 1920–1921), and the quarterly *Phylon: The Atlanta University Review of Race and Culture* (1940–1944)—were frankly instruments aimed at advancing these purposes. They also were exciting publications and remain worthwhile reading.

In a biographical and historical sense, Du Bois's editorship of *The Crisis* was the most consequential among all the magazines. Second only to that was his work with *The Horizon*, which served as the organ of the militant Niagara Movement, as the significant antecedent of *The Crisis*, and, with William Monroe Trotter's Boston *Guardian*, a powerful and vigorous opponent of the Tuskegee Machine.

The Horizon appeared in the midst of the worst period in the post-Civil War history of the Afro-American people—the era correctly called "the nadir" by the late Rayford W. Logan. Between 1890 and 1910, lynching and peonage were institutionalized. In the same period, Black men were disfranchised from Florida to Oklahoma, and Jim Crow was legalized—both actions undertaken with the blessings of the U.S. Supreme Court. Pogroms in the South and in the North were recurrent, notably those in Atlanta, Georgia (1906) and Springfield, Illinois (1908).

The ideological rationalization for this—the so-called "scientific racism" in history, anthropology, and psychology—was dominant, while popular propaganda, from such magazines as the *Saturday Evening Post* to such best-selling novels as those by Thomas Dixon, was steeped in the most blatant kind of racism. Nationally, monopoly capitalism was triumphant, and nowhere more so than in the South, to which industry (attracted by especially low wages and the relative absence of unions) was moving at a record pace. The special protegé of that class, Booker T. Washington, exerted enormous power in controlling vocal and printed expressions of opinion from Black America.

Du Bois's activities, such as pioneering in scientific sociology and history, directing the Atlanta University Studies, helping launch the Pan-African Movement in 1900, publishing, in the same year, essays critical of Washington, the stunning impact of *The Souls of Black Folk* (1903), the already noted *Moon* and Niagara efforts, in large part were aimed at thwarting the Tuskegee Machine, led by Booker T. Washington.

The *Moon*, begun in 1905 with a pittance, printed in Memphis and edited single-handedly by Du Bois while he was an overly busy professor in Atlanta, did not have significant impact and lasted but two years. It was not like Du Bois to give up, however; with him, failure existed as an encouragement to renewed effort. As the *Moon* set, a new *Horizon* was espied; with the new year its first number appeared, in January 1907.[1]

For the first two years (volumes 1–4), *The Horizon* was a pocket-size magazine (5½ in. by 4½ in.), 28 pages in length. Through 1907 it was published in Washington, in 1908 in Alexandria, Virginia, and then in 1909 until its end in Washington again. The printing was done in a shop owned by the Murray brothers, Freeman H. M. Murray (who served first as co-editor and after 1908 as assistant editor), and F. Morris Murray, the magazine's business manager. From the beginning, Lafayette M. Hershaw was associated in an editorial capacity.[2]

The magazine had severe financial difficulties throughout its existence; its three-man board received no salary. Indeed, they contributed several hundred dollars of their own scanty incomes towards maintaining the periodical. Some of the funding appeals will be found in the following pages.

At the close of 1908 it was necessary to issue a combined November/December number, which announced plans for an enlarged magazine in 1909. Du Bois's editorial in this issue urged that each subscriber find two or three new subscribers; if this did not occur, the editorial warned, the *Horizon* would expire after 1909.

In reality, the next issue (volume 5, number 1) did not appear until November 1909; it was now in an 8 in. by 11 in. format and totaled twelve double-column pages. It managed thereafter to appear each month (except for April 1910) through July 1910, when it ceased publication. By July 1910, the National Association for the Advancement of Colored People (NAACP) had been formed, Du Bois had resigned his Atlanta University position and accepted appointment to the NAACP Board and the editorship of *The Crisis*. When the latter magazine appeared in November 1910, with an original printing of 1000 copies, subscribers to *The Horizon* received *The Crisis*.

* * *

The Horizon consisted of three departments. Almost always it opened with Du Bois's "Over-Look"; this department contained news and views, as reported in leading journals and books published throughout the world, that were consequential to Black people, as well as others (especially Jews) who were subject to special insult and oppression. Usually this was followed by the "Out-Look," for which L. M. Hershaw was responsible. This department reported on domestic political developments important to Afro-Americans in particular. The issue concluded with F.H.M. Murray's "In-Look," which detailed the main contents of the preceding month's Afro-American magazines and newspapers.

---

[1]One of the few collections that possesses a complete set of the original magazine is Sterling Memorial Library at Yale University; its courtesy in supplying copies for this work is deeply appreciated.

[2]Hershaw participated in the first Atlanta University Conference conducted by Du Bois in 1898, as well as in the tenth Conference in 1905. During the years of *The Horizon*, Murray held a clerkship in the War Department in Washington, D.C. In a letter that appeared in the June 1919 issue of *The Crisis*, Murray criticized an attack upon the I.W.W. that had appeared in a *Crisis* issue earlier that year (during Du Bois's absence). Both Hershaw and Murray were among the original members of the Niagara Movement. Regrettably, neither is in R.W. Logan and M.R. Winston, eds., *A Dictionary of American Negro Biography* (1983); they merit extended biographical notice.

In the pages that follow, Du Bois's department is reprinted in full, with several exceptions. Omitted are poems and short stories by Du Bois which are reprinted in the *Creative Writings* volume of this series.[3] Also omitted are occasional signed contributions by others, such as an essay on "Negro Soldiers" by an English scholar, Dr. Frances Hoggan (May 1908).

In this volume, as in all of this series, purely typographical errors are silently corrected. The Name Index, following the main text, offers the full names of people mentioned by Du Bois, who here, as often elsewhere, provided only surnames.

Notable in this work is its manifestation of Du Bois's universality, with coverage of African and African-derived peoples, and Asian, Native American, and Jewish peoples. Du Bois's enlightened views on women are marked features of the material in *The Horizon*, as is his insistence upon the relationship between racism and male supremacy. In this connection, see in particular his passionate tribute to Ida Dean Bailey in the March 1908 issue. The *Horizon* years also marked a sharpening of Du Bois's political and economic radicalism. This is strikingly shown in his advocacy of political independence for Black people and his growing sympathy towards Socialism.

Several of the essays in *The Horizon* are of major consequence—notably his series on politics, including his call, in 1908, to break away from the Republican Party, and his prophetic projection of increasing weight to the Black electorate. Important, too, are certain speeches by Du Bois, especially his address to the (white) YMCA in New York City (March 1910, article no. 29) and to graduates of the Colored High School of Baltimore (June 1910, article no. 30). There he told the youngsters: "The races who are content with slavery are slaves, the animals who are willing to cringe and follow are dogs, and the men who are satisfied are dead."

Notable also is the material on the Du Bois–Washington controversy; in this connection observe particularly the partial text of Du Bois's pungent speech, in Hershaw's "Out-look" section of the May 1910 issue, and herein reprinted (in the Editor's Note to article no. 29). Du Bois's suggestion (November/December 1908 issue, article no. 23) to vivify the 1900 effort at a Pan-African movement foretells what was to be a major component of his astonishing career.

Unique for this period is Du Bois's bibliography of books and articles relevant to racism, colonialism, and anti-Semitism. Some of the references will surprise and enlighten even the most expert. Note, as examples, the article cited in the *North American* for December 1906, urging an end to Jim Crow in the United States Army, and the appearance, in October 1908, of an essay discussing consumer cooperation among Black people—a matter of the greatest interest to Du Bois, especially in the 1930's. Furthermore, Du Bois's high recommendation of the novel entitled *The Stigma*, written by a Mrs. Selkirk and published in Boston in 1906, might well justify a discovery of that quite forgotten book.

The reader, then, has before him or her a significant slice of Du Bois's literary effort and insightful commentary upon an important moment in Afro-American history.

HERBERT APTHEKER

---

[3]Du Bois, W.E.B. *Creative Writings by W.E.B. Du Bois: A Pageant, Poems, Short Stories, and Playlets.* Edited by Herbert Aptheker. (White Plains, N.Y. Kraus-Thomson Organization Ltd., 1985).

Writings in Periodicals
Edited by W.E.B. Du Bois

Selections from
THE HORIZON

1

The Over-Look

THE MAGAZINES

The Atlanta Tragedy: From the Point of View of the Whites, by John Temple Graves; from the Negro point of View, by W. E. Burghardt DuBois, WORLD TODAY, November.

A Southern View of the Negro Problem. Stanhope Sams. ECLECTIC, November.

The Negro Problem: The North and the Negro, by Fergus Crane; Long Views and Short on White and Black, by Sidney Olivier. ECLECTIC, December.

The Terrible Story of the Congo. Robert E. Park. The author charges that during the past twenty years King Leopold of Belgium has sacrificed fifteen million lives in the Congo Free State. EVERYBODY'S, December.

Out of the Heart. An anonymous letter from a Southern woman about the increasing antagonism between the white people of the South and the Negro. AMERICAN, December.

The South Africa Constitution. By H. W. Massingham. An account of England's effort to frame a yoke that will gall neither Boer nor Briton, Kaffir nor Oriental. THE WORLD'S WORK, December.

A Farmer's College on Wheels. By Booker T. Washington. WORLD'S WORK, December.

Caste—the Curse of India. By Chas. E. Russell. How the great empire's ancient social system is breaking down the country. COSMOPOLITAN, December.

The New China. By Hon. John W. Foster, formerly Secretary of State. Mr. Foster describes the transformation that has taken place in China during the last several years. Customs that have been unalterable for 3,000 years have been cast away and a new education and a new spirit have begun to animate this most populous and conservative of nations. NATIONAL GEOGRAPHIC MAGAZINE, December.

The White Man's Zone in Africa. Samuel P. Verner. WORLD'S WORK, November.

Last of the Indian Treaties. Duncan C. Scott. SCRIBNER'S, November.

Christmas among the Indians, Francis E. Leupp. LADIES' HOME JOURNAL, December.

An Old Plantation Christmas. Martha McCulloch-Williams. SUBURBAN LIFE, December.

California and the Japanese Treaty. Chas. C. Hyde. GREEN BAG, December.

Reminiscences of a Long Life. Second Series, Part II. Carl Schurz. McCLURE'S, December.

From *The Horizon: A Journal of the Color Line* 1 (January 1907): 2–10.

———

Mr. Ray Stannard Baker is about to commence a series of articles on the Negro problem, in the American Magazine. It is to be sincerely hoped that they will not be as superficial as his articles on lynching.

———

One God-send to the American Negro is the collapse of Tom Watson's Magazine or at least of the editor of it.

———

Joel Chandler Harris is to commence the publication of a magazine called "Uncle Remus' Magazine." Whatever there is of genius in Joel Chandler Harris is due entirely to the Negro.

SUBSCRIPTION

Every Negro American ought to subscribe for a number of good papers. First of all, of course, should come the race papers: the GUARDIAN, $1.50 a year, and the VOICE at a dollar a year; then comes the intelligence of things that are happening outside our own race; first, there is the daily paper—happy is the black man who can take a daily like the New York EVENING POST—the TRANSCRIPT used to be as good but it has fallen from grace since O'Brien took charge. Then come the weekly papers which loom large these days. Above all, every Negro should subscribe for the New York INDEPENDENT. It is the bravest and the fairest in its stand on the Negro problem. Next, perhaps, comes the LITERARY DIGEST. The Negro has always received fair treatment in this paper; $3.00 cannot be better spent than in getting the year's general view of literature and news and opinions which this paper gives. On the other hand, there are certain weekly papers which the Negro ought to steer clear of; the OUTLOOK for instance, which represents militant hypocrisy in ethics and literature, is doubly unfair to the Negro because it pretends friendship. COLLIER'S tries to be as unfair as it reasonably can be, with occasional jolts from the counting room. Of the monthly magazines, colored men should beware of SCRIBNER'S and the CENTURY, especially the former. The CENTURY has lapsed into fairness now and then. Take HARPER'S if you want to hear nothing of the race problem—they are afraid of it—but don't under any circumstances take HARPER'S WEEKLY. One of the best papers for colored men is the WEST AFRICAN MAIL. It costs a good deal—$6.00 a year—but it is the best paper published for articles on the African situation.

BOOKS

This year has not been prolific with books of especial interest to the American Negro yet there are some which we cannot omit. Perhaps the greatest book of the year is Merriam's THE NEGRO AND THE NATION, written with fairness and considerable research. After that comes a novel, THE STIGMA, written by Mrs. Selkirk. Little has been said about this novel. The press tried to bury it but every colored man should buy one. Turner of Boston published it and it is a brave, outspoken story of the South. A little outside the race problem there are books of the holiday season one ought to have, as for instance the new edition of Cable's OLD CREOLE DAYS. Of the general novels, read by all means Mrs. DeLand's AWAKENING OF ELEANOR† RITCHIE. Read, too, CONISTON, but don't bother about LADY BALTIMORE. Owen Wister doesn't care much for black folk. Of distinctively Negro American literature, by far the greatest thing of the season is Braithwaite's ELIZABETHAN POETRY. I have not seen it yet but it is spoken highly of and it is an essay in serious literature by the greatest Negro American poet. Mr. Washington has also published two books: one, a LIFE OF FREDERICK DOUGLASS.

CONGO

It is a long story, a shameful story. There lay the land. There came men telling the world the wonderful things they were going to do for it; they lifted up their hands toward Heaven and said: we will save these black folk; we will give our lives for them. Here shall be a land of peace, plenty and development guaranteed by the civilized world. But the devil came also in the shape of Leopold of Belgium and he slew 15,000,000 human beings and out of their blood he is today walking away with a loot of millions and millions of stolen blood money. He seems too, about to get away with it. Only one thing is pleasant to us who stand and think and that is that the loot, so far as he is concerned, is going to stop. To be sure he is bringing America into it. We wanted to bring America before. We wanted America to lift up her hands to make him stop but America would not. Now, however, America is entering in a characteristic way as money makers, as heirs to the looting and the stealing which has gone on so long. A great syndicate with Ryan and Rockefeller has bought interests there. Will America let them do as their predecessors have done? No. The day of reckoning is coming. Watch it.

INDIA

There is a land of dark men far across the sea which is of interest to us. The land of India, the land, perhaps, from whence our fore-fathers came, or whither certainly in some prehistoric time they wandered. There a white race has conquered brown men. The brown men have lain for years inert, but now they are coming to life. They are looking. They are listening. They are asking. Two parties are there; in some ways resembling the two parties among us. One party says: wait, look for a chance, take all the English give us, and gradually achieve freedom; the other party says: no, freedom now, we are men. In this case I am not sure with which party I agree. The situation is complicated. One thing I do rejoice at, that is that both parties want freedom. With us it looks as though somebody did not want freedom, as though they were actually afraid of it.

ROOSEVELT

If the truth must be told, Theodore Roosevelt does not like black folk. He has no faith in them. I do not think that he really ever knew a colored man intimately as a friend. The colored men he knows are or have been politicians or men who have humored his whims. Consequently he feels in no way drawn to the black population of the United States, as he is drawn, for instance, toward the South. He reaped chagrin and the criticism of the South some years ago. Immediately he let the Negro go. It was easy to jump at such a chance as he saw at Brownsville to deal him a blow and at the same time to do the South a favor. Without doubt he thought he was doing justice. The trouble is, and the crime lay, in the impulsive, unthinking judgment. Yet in this respect, he is not different from his fellows. He is an American. The pity of it is, we expected more.

SHEA

A more disgraceful attempt to discredit, maim and abuse black working men than that of Shea and his bribed Myrmidons was never seen. The disgrace of it all was the ease with which white Chicago succumbed, believed and mobbed and harmed Negroes; it is the old tale: organized attempt to steal the black man's bread and butter as true in Atlanta and Chattanooga as in Chicago and even truer.

MOONSHINE

Yes, it was moonshine—with all its soft seductiveness and lure. They were two young men, poor and inexperienced but thoroughly honest and full of work.‡ I felt like helping them—rather I felt like working with them, albeit in ways I was as inexperienced as they. We needed capital. I sought it. "Subsidy" yelled the Cheerful Idiot, who knows what subsidy is. No, Tom and Jerry, it was precisely that which we refused. Well, we started, we had our little feverish trial and failed. It was a good, honest failure without frills and excuses and without dishonor. I was sorry for the boys—it was very bitter for them. As for me—why, here goes again. Yes, it was Moon-shine.

EDITOR'S NOTES
†This should read Helena.

‡Reference is to *The Moon,* edited by Du Bois; assisting were E. L. Simon and Harry H. Pace. It was published in Memphis from December 1905 to July 1906; only two issues seem to have survived.

2

The Over-Look

"Awake then put on Thy strength, O Zion!
Put on Thy Beautiful Robes!"

THE MAGAZINES

The faithful may find sustenance and confusion in the following articles:

M. F. Steele's Condemnation of the Color Line in the Army. He points out that there is
no place where Negro soldiers can be stationed despite their efficiency. Therefore, he says, abolish the Jim Crow regiments and let Negroes enlist in all
regiments. NORTH AMERICAN, December 21;

R.E. Park continues the horrible *Story of Congo.* EVERYBODY'S, January.

C. C. Adams points out the *Unknown Parts of Africa* and other continents. HARPER'S,
January.

The Biological Bulletin of the University of Chicago, (December) has an article on
Ants by C. H. Turner, one of us.

Washington Gladden speaks a brave, true word for *Color Justice.* AMERICAN,
January.

Immigration and the Negro, W. L. Fleming. WORLD TODAY, January.

Golden Rule in Atlanta, B. T. Washington. OUTLOOK, December 15.

Soldiers of common good. OUTLOOK, Dec. 29.

Curse of the Congo. CURRENT LITERATURE, January.

King Leopold's Self-Defense. OUTLOOK, December 22.

Other articles of lesser interest are:

What Japanese Exclusion would mean: O. Howes. NORTH AMERICAN, January 4.

The Jews: H. Fishberg. POPULAR SCIENCE MONTHLY, December.

Natural History of American Morals: F. H. Giddings. TIMES MAGAZINE, January.

I ought to have mentioned last month the SPRINGFIELD REPUBLICAN as
a staunch friend of the Negro American in his struggles.

FRANCE

France is civilized. The *Petit Parisien* has had a newspaper *enquête* of fifteen
million votes on the relative prominence of Frenchmen of the nineteenth century.
Here is the order of voting:

From *The Horizon: A Journal of the Color Line* 1 (February 1907): 3–4, 6–10.

1. Pasteur; the scientist.
2. Victor Hugo; the writer.
3. Gambetta; the revolutionist.
4. Napoleon I; the conqueror.
8. Dumas; the writer.
13. Zola; the writer.
16. Bernhardt; the actress.

Here is deference and respect shown to knowledge, genius, and poverty; the crowning, above all, of the alleviation of human suffering; and finally in the person of the Negro Frenchman, Dumas, absolute indifference to the colorline; and in the person of a great actress, to the false barrier of sex. France is civilized.

SOCIALIST OF THE PATH

I am a Socialist-of-the-Path. I do not believe in the complete socialization of the means of production—the entire abolition of private property in capital—but the Path of Progress and common sense certainly leads to a far greater ownership of the public wealth for the public good than is now the case. I do not believe that government can carry on private business as well as private concerns, but I do believe that most of the human business called private is no more private than God's blue sky, and that we are approaching a time when railroads, coal mines and many factories can and ought to be run by the public for the public. This is the way, as I see it, that the path leads and I follow it gladly and hopefully.

NEGRO AND SOCIALISM

In the socialistic trend thus indicated lies the one great hope of the Negro American. We have been thrown by strange historic reasons into the hands of the capitalists hitherto. We have been objects of dole and charity, and despised accordingly. We have been made tools of oppression against the workingman's cause—the puppets and playthings of the idle rich. Fools! We must awake! Not in a renaissance among ourselves of the evils of Get and Grab—not in private hoarding, squeezing and cheating, lies our salvation, but rather in that larger ideal of human brotherhood, equality of opportunity and work not for wealth but for Weal—here lies our shining goal. This goal the Socialists with all their extravagance and occasional foolishness have more stoutly followed than any other class and thus far we must follow them. Our natural friends are not the rich but the poor, not the great but the masses, not the employers but the employees. Our good is not wealth, power, oppression and snobbishness, but helpfulness, efficiency, service and self-respect. Watch the Socialists. We may not follow them and agree with them in all things. I certainly do not. But in trend and ideal they are the salt of this present earth.

INDIA

The speech of Naoroji before the National Congress of India was worthy of men who want to be free. He said:

> The peasants of Russia are fit for and obtained the *Duma* from the greatest autocrat in the world, and the leading statesman, the Prime Minister, of the free

British Empire proclaimed to the world, "The *Duma* is dead ; long live the *Duma!*" Surely the fellow-citizens of that statesman and the free citizens of that Empire by birth-right and pledged rights are far more entitled to self-government, a constitutional representative system, than the peasants of Russia. I do not despair. It is futile to tell me that we must wait till all the people are ready. The British people did not so wait for their Parliament. We are not allowed to be fit for 150 years. We can never be fit till we actually undertake the work and the responsibility. While China in the east and Persia in the west of Asia are awakening, and Japan has already awakened, and Russia is struggling for emancipation— and all of them despotisms—can the free citizens of the British Indian Empire continue to remain subject to despotism, the people who were among the first civilizers of the world? The modern world owes no little gratitude to these early civilizers of the human race. Are the descendants of the earliest civilizers to remain, in the present times of spreading emancipation, under a barbarous system of despotism, unworthy of British instincts, principles, and civilization?

The dark world awakens to life and articulate speech. Courage, comrades!

AUSTRIA

Austria goes forward to universal suffrage while we go backward to the rule of the Clique, the Gang and the Despot. We read too in the London TIMES that the Galician Jews are organizing for political action and the TIMES adds:

> This laudable example might with advantage be imitated by the Jews in other parts of Austria. In this country the Jew will never be respected, until he ceases to be ashamed of his race, and seeks to exercise his political influence in the light of day. Hitherto the Jews of Austria have preferred to masquerade as members of other races preferably as "Germans," and to exercise political influence by methods that have rendered the growth of Anti-Semitism comprehensible, if not justifiable. The Galician Jews are warmly to be congratulated upon setting a good example to their fellow Semites elsewhere.

So much for "gum-shoe" and "back door" and "conciliating" methods !

LAGOS

The exploitation of the native West African by the combined concentrated capitalistic methods of Europe goes on apace. The Lagos STANDARD says:

> In the commercial world, trade, as has been pointed out before now, is almost entirely out of the hands of the Native, from which field of enterprise he has been practically ousted by the keen and ruinous competition of the big European firms. The industrial or agricultural line is what now offers him any prospect of gaining a fair livelihood, and even this field is being so much invaded by Europeans that there is no telling how soon it, too, will be monopolised by the foreigner, and the Native relegated to the position of "hewers of wood and drawers of water," leaving to the white man the agreeable part of reaping the rich profits.

Is this mere native inefficiency? Nonsense. It is the helplessness of unorganized and disfranchised labor before organized, ruthless and ruling capital backed by greed.

3

The Over-Look

"Ho, every one that thirsteth, come ye to the waters, and he that hath no money; come ye, buy, and eat; yea, come, buy wine and milk without money and without price."
                                                                    Isaiah 55:1

BOOKS

The best book·of the month is Finot's RACE PREJUDICE, (Dutton, $3) followed by Olivier's WHITE CAPITAL AND COLORED LABOR, England; (1 s.) They ridicule the exaggerated pretensions of "superior" races and defend the mulatto. After these read:

Dennett: THE BLACK MAN'S MIND;	Macmillan.
Lloyd: UGANDA TO KHARTOUM;	Dutton, $3.
Addams: NEWER IDEALS OF PEACE;	Macmillan, $1.25
Thomas: SEX AND SOCIETY;	University of Chicago, $1.50

PERIODICALS

The month's magazines and their treatment of Us will make the Man of March, 2907 to shriek with laughter. We shriek now, but not wholly with laughter.

The bravest word is Well's "Race Prejudice" in the INDEPENDENT (February 14) reviewing Finot and Olivier. Do you take the INDEPENDENT? TAKE IT. Baker of the AMERICAN has at least learned that you cannot know the Negro in a minute, hence his March article consists of two pictures and a postponement. The LITERARY DIGEST of February 16 discusses Negrophobia in the Atlanta NEWS and the unfortunate Ralph Tyler incident. The REVIEW OF REVIEWS for February has Adams on "Civilizing Work of Modern Christian Missions," showing Negro artisans in Africa. Stone, who is living in affluence on Negro labor, discounts it generally in favor of Italians. In the March number is a plan of Jamestown. Behold the poor Negro side-show three-quarters of a mile from the main exposition, away from everybody and everything, beyond the midway, next to the woods and camping ground where white soldiers can insult colored women to their heart's content. Are you going?

The OUTLOOK (March 2) pleads for justice toward the Filipinos, and Lyman Abbot's heart just aches for Russia:
                "I du believe in Freedom's cause
                Ez fur ez Payris is!"

From *The Horizon: A Journal of the Color Line* 1 (March 1907): 3–10.

8

The REVUE ECONOMIQUE INTERNATIONALE of Belgium has in the November number a long and sympathetic article on the Negro Workingmen in the United States.†

Mr. E. G. Murphy, who attacked the public sometime since with a proposal to repeal the 15th Amendment and afterward repented, tells of the "task of the Southern leader" in the January SEWANEE REVIEW. He foresees the turning of the Negro from farming to industry and deplores the increasing "evil Negro leadership" which preaches "grievances and fostering of hate." In short, he wants the worm to quit turning.

The ILLUSTRATED LONDON NEWS of February 2 and 9 has excellent pictures of Jamaicans and of the young black king of Uganda.

Other articles are:

Caste in Various Countries. By Charles Edward Russell. A first-hand study of this pernicious social system in various countries. COSMOPOLITAN, (February).

The problem of the Southern cotton-mill. By Mary Applewhite Bacon. The author visited many of the principal mills in a personal investigation of the child-labor problem. ATLANTIC, (February).

Negro Education, Progress of. H. B. Frissell. SOUTH ATLANTIC QUARTERLY, (January).

Congo, Belgian Rule on the. S. P. Verner. WORLD'S WORK, (February).

African Wilderness, Wiring the. S. S. Burton. TECHNICAL WORLD, (February).

India's Awakening : the Swadeshi Movement. Yotrinda Mohan Bose. OUTLOOK, (January 19).

Kongo Evidence, Suppressed. John H. Harris. INDEPENDENT, (January 10).

Indians, The, and Oklahoma. Henry S. Brown. OUTLOOK, (January 19).

The South and its Chief Problem, By "V. E. P. N." An elaborate review of the Negro question, by a prominent college professor. TIMES MAGAZINE, (March).

The Destruction of our Indian. By Frederick Monsen. What civilization is doing to extinguish an ancient race by taking away its arts, industries, and religion. CRAFTSMAN, (March).

Shaping the Future of the Indians. By Forbes Lindsay. What is being done to provide occupation for the Indian. WORLD TODAY, (March).

Filipinos, a Plea for the. Gen W. H. Carter. NORTH AMERICAN, (February 15).

Negro Question, Acuteness of. William D. Jelks. NORTH AMERICAN, (February 15).

Race Problem in Washington, from a Negro Standpoint. INDEPENDENT, (January 24).

Race riots and Lynch Laws: A Northern Professor's view. J. E. Cutler, A Southern Lawyer's view. Hooper Alexander. OUTLOOK, (February 2).

The Maoris of New Zealand. By Le Comte de Courte. A description of an interesting dark race. NATIONAL GEOGRAPHIC MAGAZINE, (March).

HEARKEN, THEODORE ROOSEVELT

Theodore Roosevelt, this is the chance of your career. You have done wrong.‡ That is not strange. So have others, high and low, thousands and millions before you. You have acted hastily, impulsively and doggedly. So all men act who think strongly and feel deeply. But slowly, surely the wrong you have done a hundred black men and their ten million fellows has struggled doubtingly, determinedly to the light and sits today in silent judgment on your soul. I will not say that the 25th Infantry have absolutely proven their entire innocence, but I do say, and the whole country agrees, that they have raised a doubt as to their guilt—a doubt so real, so firm, so reasonable that no court in Christendom would convict them in the face of it. You have convicted them. You thought them guilty. Their guilt is today unproven. You know it is unproven. You know that their innocence is so near proven that the nation sits dumb before their testimony. The nation is watching you. The black millions are waiting. Theodore Roosevelt, are you an honest man? If you are, speak!

JOURNEYING

I have been journeying, and voices and faces have passed before me like the mirage of whispering winds. Souls, I have seen faintly, as perfume flies, and bodies beautiful, alluring, ugly, curious. I feel as though I had dipped me in the deeper world and thrown my naked form athwart foam-crested waves, kicked my feet against the muddied eddies of the shallow pool and the dark waters curling, lapping, cursing had clasped themselves behind me and forgotten. I have not forgotten, shall not forget, the whispering sea of dark, kindly faces at Bethel, Chicago; the colder, scanter curiousness at the University; the cosmopolitan catholicity of Hull House. I remember the great round pit of Carnegie Hall in New York and the silent, black coated throng that lined its floor, and the sweet, merry girl faces of St. Faith's. Vaulted churches pass before me and the churchly, staid and doubting, half hostile audience of Trinity in old Philadelphia. Was I not glad to return unto mine own and see the brown and smiling welcome of a thousand faces in Baltimore and sit at meat with them that yearn in the Capital? Then shuddering as I always do, I plunged across the line into Egypt to the warmer, sweeter glow of Durham and the students of Benedict. And in the end, as ever, back to Thee, and Peace— and War, Atlanta.

BACK-TALK

Readers, gentle and otherwise, will receive, all courtesy and consideration whenever they feel like talking back. Please do so.

"Why do you stick in pins when dignified criticism would accomplish much more? The style of THE HORIZON is unworthy of you. The idea is good, but the style is atrocious. 'To the woods with it.' "—Alabama.

"You ought, it seems to me, to be careful how you direct the attention of your supporters to the adoption of any socialistic principle whatever as a means to an end, to say nothing of the evils which are likely to follow in the train of their association or identification with any such body of agitators.

"It is true that you have qualified your remarks by the proviso that 'we may not follow them and agree with them in all things'; but even this seems not to be safe enough if law and order is to be upheld. Appealing therefore to your knowledge of human nature, may I ask if you think in all seriousness that Negroes will escape the virus of socialism (popular) even if they are careful to assimilate its ideals(?) and reject the chaff?"—Minnesota.

INDIAN

The new U. S. Senator, Charles Curtis of Kansas, is a half-blood Indian, and the Montgomery [Ala.] ADVERTISER defends the man and mixture thus:

"The bird that fouls its own nest is the proper simile for the American who denies the American Indian of pure or mixed blood the opportunity to fit himself for places that he has proved his ability to fill."

Is the South utterly devoid of humor, or was the editor out?

NOTES

The Peabody fund of $1,000,000 left for education in the South has been given to a Tennessee institution which bars black Southerners. Mr. Peabody is still dead.

Judge Thomas of Alabama, although graciously allowing the Negroes five-sixths of all the southern murders, still is sure that the Negro and the immigrant are not responsible for the excess of homicides in this land.

> The investigation of the Brownsville affair by the Senate Committee has been one-sided thus far, but it goes very far to show that the soldiers should have been tried by court-martial, where all facts could have been carefully tested. It looks very much as if not a single Negro fired a gun, and we shall be pleased if this is proved. —N.Y. INDEPENDENT, Feb. 21, Editorial.

EDITOR'S NOTES

†This refers to Du Bois's article, "L'Ouvrier nègre en Amérique," in the magazine cited (4: 298–348).

‡The reference is to the so-called Brownsville Episode of August 1906. Militant black troops of the famous 25th Infantry Regiment attacked a section of the Texas town, killing one white person, wounding another and injuring the chief of police. In November, on the basis of an inspector's report, President Roosevelt dismissed the entire battalion without honor. Protests against this summary action lasted for decades; the dishonorable discharges were finally rescinded by Congress in 1972. See: Ann J. Lane, *The Brownsville Affair* (1973).

4

The Over-Look

THE CONSERVATIVE

"I do not want to fly," said he,
  "I only want to squirm!"
And he dropped his wings dejectedly,
  But still his voice was firm:
"I do not want to be a fly!
  I want to be a worm!"

Stetson.

MAGAZINES

We are not quite so popular this month and yet we occupy considerable space. S.S. McClure for reasons best known to his pocket forwards Nelson Page's Anti-Negro campaign. He writes me, "We have had a good many requests to print replies to his article, but have uniformly refused because we do not wish to open our pages to a controversy." A controversy is indeed dangerous to a flimsy argument. Major Robert M. Moton begins his interesting life-tale in the WORLD'S WORK (April). May he have the courage to tell the truth and not gloss it and doctor it for copperhead consumption. The article of the month is Baker's Atlanta Riot in the AMERICAN. Because of his initial twist in those unfair lynching articles the author always exaggerates Negro crime and what he does in this line his illustrator sadly supplements. On the whole, however, his article strives for fairness and is very good indeed. Read it.

This is the Month's Menu:

Negro Question: The Great American Problem. Thos. Nelson Page. McClure, March.
Slavery in the South Today. Richard Barry. Cosmopolitan, March.
Negro, The, as an American Soldier. William H. Head. World To-Day, March.
East Africa, The British Protectorate in. Lord Hindlip. Eclectic, March.
Negro, Autobiography of a. Part I. Major Robert M. Moton. World's Work, April.
Color Line, Following the. Part I. Atlanta Race Riot and After. Ray Stannard Baker.
    American, April.
Lynchings, Facts as to. W. D. P. Bliss. Homiletic Review, April.
Race Problem—Where it has Solved itself. Eliza F. Andrews. Century, April.
Liberia. National Geographic Magazine, April.
Africa Fifty Years Hence. Samuel P. Verner. World's Work, April.

From *The Horizon: A Journal of the Color Line* 1 (April 1907): 3–9.

Cuban Negro, The. R. I. Bullard, NORTH AMERICAN REVIEW, March 16.
Caste in America, Growth of. Chas. E. Russell. COSMOPOLITAN, March.
Kingston, The Aftermath of. Broughton Brandenburg. WORLD TODAY, March.
Ku Klux Klan, Reminiscences of the. Sally Royce Weir. METROPOLITAN, April.

The DIAL says of Braithwaite's interesting study of Magazine poetry:

"Mr. Braithwaite has already done good work for the cause of poetry—witness his recent
excellent compilation of 'Elizabethan Verse'—and his authority as a critic is not
contemptible."

And moreover he's colored.

BOOKS

Buy books. Do not merely read them but buy them, own them, make them
yours. Do not simply use libraries, but buy books. Magazines? Of course. In fact
we are magazine-mad—a magazine-devouring nation and our mental digestion
suffers thereby. Newspapers? Of cruel necessity; but of all festering abominations,
away with the Sunday newspaper. It is an imp of Hell and child of the Devil, not
because it is published on Sunday (for it isn't) but because it is hodge-podge of lie,
gossip, twaddle and caricature. It ruins our Sundays, corrupts our morals, poisons
our children and gives us headaches. Away with it and read books. A book is a
serious thought-out theme written to live. Therefore buy books. The more books
we buy the more books written to our liking will be published for others to buy
and ponder. Buy books.

AFRICA

In the Transvaal under the new constitution the Dutch premier, Botha, has
already taken up, "from the Boer point of view, a sympathetic attitude towards the
natives—that is, he would treat them fairly and even generously, as members of a
subordinate race, but not allow them ever to be more than decently attired and
well-behaved servants in the white men's homes and farms and workshops, toiling
for a moderate wage and protected from active persecution, but prevented from
being their own masters, acquiring land or enjoying political rights of any sort. In
practice, if not in theory, and whatever it may have been in former days, Boer
tyranny over natives has come to be better than mineowners tyranny, but it is tyranny
for all that."

The state of affairs in Natal, where "all the mischief done during the months
of 'martial law' last year is being systematized and turned to account under the
pretence of a pacific carrying out of the ordinary law," is deplorable.

In Lugard's last report we learn that Nigeria, a West African protectorate, has
260,000 square miles and 9 million inhabitants. He says: "The introduction of new
food plants, and of better modes of cultivation, the access to markets at present
closed to them, where food may be bought in exchange for silvan products of
commercial value, the inauguration of industrial missions, and finally, in extreme
cases, the direct assistance of government, are benefits which it is worth while to
acquire at the cost of a light taxation, and the obligation to cease from outrages
and war."

The outlook for reform in Congo is gloomy. "It is the manifest policy of the

Congo government and its supporters to do everything in their power to dawdle and confuse the proceedings of the Commission, in the hope of delaying for some time, if not altogether averting by devices as clever as any that they have successfully employed hitherto, the retribution that seems otherwise inevitable." Belgium is seeking annexation but England will hardly allow this. The *Cape Times* is exposing the Portugese slave trade in Southeast and Southwest Africa. "The men embarking on this business of cruelty are mostly Portugese mulattos. These men grow enormously rich on what they call their 'black ivory trade'!" This slave-trading is not much better than the South African. "Indeed the whole system of labor-recruiting for the supply of Kaffirs for the Transvaal mines is, albeit a mild one, a form of slave-trading. Much graver allegations are made, moreover, apparently on strong grounds, against those who carry on an extensive and illicit traffic between the Katanga district of the Congo State and the Mozambique market."

The American Board of Commissioners for Foreign Missions who have withdrawn all their colored missionaries from Africa are respectfully asked to send them to Belgium, England, Portgual and—Georgia.

UNKNOWN

The ignorance which white America shows of Black America is both laughable and pitiable. For instance, the colored people publish over two hundred, probably 250, papers, including 6 monthly magazines; and yet the genial editor of WHAT'S IN THE MAGAZINES remarks: "THE HORIZON, ('a journal of the color line') is a little monthly publication written and printed by Negroes, the first number of which has just appeared. There are now no less than three periodicals published in the interest of the colored race in America, the other two being the VOICE of Chicago and the GUARDIAN of Boston." He knows naught even of the CONSERVATOR of his own Chicago, the doughtiest champion, next the GUARDIAN, of the rights of Negroes, and edited by an unpurchaseable man.† Then too there's our good friend the LITERARY DIGEST: the last number translates from the REVUE SCIENTIFIQUE of Paris some remarkable observations of ants by C. H. Turner; blissfully ignorant that the BIOLOGICAL BULLETIN, of the University of Chicago, had the original article in plain English; and also unconscious, we suspect, that Turner is a Negro who just received his Ph. D., *magna cum laude* at the University of Chicago. But the climax was capped by the Southern white woman who protested to the LADIES' HOME JOURNAL: "Don't let———portray Southern music—he's a Negro. *Cole and Johnson* can do this but *No Negro can!*" So it goes. We shall know each other better when the mists have rolled away.

Editor's Note
†At that time, the editor was J. Max Barber, who had been editor of *The Voice of the Negro* in Atlanta. Barber was forced to move due to the 1906 pogrom in that city. By 1908 Barber was replaced by a Booker T. Washington man, Sandy W. Trice. The *Conservator* ceased publication in 1910.

5

The Over-Look

THE HIGHEST WORK

Beloved, let us love so well,
Our work shall still be better for our love,
And still our love be sweeter for our work.
Elizabeth Barrett Browning

MAGAZINES

This month read the AMERICAN—a fine brave article by a man who has learned to capitalize *"Negro"* in one short month and read also the April SOUTH ATLANTIC QUARTERLY.

The Clash of the Races in a Southern City. By Ray Stannard Baker. This second article in Mr. Baker's series, "Following the Color Line," is a first hand investigation of conditions in Atlanta soon after the recent race riots. Illustrated. AMERICAN, May.

Hindu Invasion: A New Immigration Problem. Fred Lockley. PACIFIC MONTHLY, May.

Jewish Immigrant: How Cared for at New York. A.S. Isaacs. WORLD TODAY, May.

Lynching in the United States. Jas. E. Cutler. SOUTH ATLANTIC QUARTERLY, April.

Negro Problem, Need of a Southern Program on the. John E. White. SOUTH ATLANTIC QUARTERLY, April.

The Silent South. John Carlisle Kilgo. SOUTH ATLANTIC QUARTERLY, April.

Kimberly (So. Africa) Diamond Mines, The. W. G. FitzGerald. WORLD TODAY, May.

A BOOK

A book to read and ponder is *Sex and Society* by Wm. I. Thomas. Mr. Thomas says:

> In the chapter on the "Mind of Woman and the Lower Races" I was represented as saying that the mind of woman was on the same plane as that of the savage, and essentially unimprovable. What I did say and devoted my whole argument to showing, was that the human mind is essentially the same pattern in all races, and in both sexes and that differences between the lower races and the white were cultural rather than organic, intelligence being dependent on the richness of suggestion and the patterns of interest prevailing in the group.

From *The Horizon: A Journal of the Color Line* 1 (May 1907): 3–10.

If this is true, it is very easy to understand why the lower races, which are geographically separated from us do not make the same show of intelligence as ourselves. And I point out also that women, on account of traditions and constraints which have grown up about them, do not possess the freedom most favorable to the development of intelligence. They have first-rate minds, but their interests are usually trivial, and their mental life necessarily remains trivial.

So far as I am advocating anything, I am advocating the full participation of woman in intellectual and scientific life. Society has, so to speak, a larger plant than it is using. It is composed of two sexes, about numerically equal, and of about equal natural ability, but it is not seriously using half its plant. I have suggested that it should add to the intelligence of its men the intelligence also of its women.

(University of Chicago Press, price $1.65.)

THE LASH

I remember my first knowing of the man.† It was about 1883, while I was a lad in the High School. I became agent for his paper and wrote crude little news notes from our town. He wrote me an encouraging letter—a good long sympathetic letter. That letter I shall not forget. No matter how far the writer has fallen and grovelled in the dust, I shall ever remember that hand of help. He worked on. His fierce brave voice made men of the nation hearken, even while it scared them. "A dangerous Negro," they said, "muzzle him." Then his voice became bitter, wild and strained and his own people joined the critics and deserted him. Temptations gathered: drink, women, debt; he staggered downward. The Arch-Tempter came, smooth-tongued and cynical, with gold: "I have a commission from the Gods-that-be to buy your soul." And the man, bitter at those who had criticized and deserted and refused to support him, mortgaged his Soul and Home to Hell. His slavery began—a bitter, cringing, maddening serfdom. His soul—that fierce old untamed soul—lashed him. Ever and again he breaks forth in fury; flashes in fierce denunciation, cynical fury or eloquent silence—then the smooth cold gold drops on his brow and he slinks cowed and trembling into his hired kennel. O, it is pitiable; thrice pitiable in a day when as never before his voice and pen are needed in the madness of the battle. And yet I cannot attack him. I receive his curious mad jibes silently. Why ? because the fault is ours as well as his. Who refused to hold up his hands ? Who refused his wiser youthful leadership? Who withheld the money and bread and clothes due him and his suffering family? We did. Shall we crucify him today for his venality, his weakness, his unbridled passions, his tottering over-aged manhood? No, rather let us bow our heads, for his shame and failure are ours. The lash that goads him, goads us, O Unfortunate!

MARCH 25TH, 1907

One hundred years ago in March, the first step toward the abolition of Negro Slavery was taken by the passage of Wilberforce's bill abolishing the English Slave Trade. The *Niagara Movement* will celebrate this event at its annual August meeting. Meantime in England and Africa the celebration has already occurred. At Westminster Abbey, March 25:

No less than three hundred people were present. The Very Revd Dean Robinson, who with Venerable Archdeacon Wilberforce received us at 2 p. m., within the Jerusalem Chamber, said he was pleased to greet us inside the historic Abbey. Leading us to the monument of Wilberforce, we passed the grave of Livingstone which he said should be of interest to us. Before Wilberforce's monument he said that it was well to remember that Harriet Beecher Stowe, authoress of Uncle Tom's Cabin, remarked that she always had consolation in the thought of what these great and good men had done; and he was pleased to observe that Archdeacon Wilberforce and Sir Thomas F. Buxton and Canon Dillvy, direct descendents of the great abolitionists, were present with us. In the words of Stowe the Dean concluded "Remember what God has done; remember that this great curse of slavery has gone forever." On Wilberforce's monument a wreath was placed in the name of Sierra Leone, Lagos, and other places in Africa by Mr. A. B. C. Merriman-Labor of Lincoln's Inn. The Rev. C. Macaulay of the U. M. F. C. College, Manchester, placed one there on behalf of Africans in America and the West Indies, and Barrister J. Wilfred Maxwell laid a third for Africans in the United Kingdom. Mr. J. Eugene Dawson, some-time Comptroller of Customs, Sierra Leone, through his proxy, Mr. J. L. Franklin of the Great Ormond Street Homeopathic Hospital, placed a fourth on the grave of Wilberforce. The other wreath-bearers were Messrs I. E. Barnes a civil engineer, Samuel Lewis and J. Otomba Payne of the Inner Temple, G. C. Montioa of Makeking and Lincoln's Inn, E. A. Osora of Sierra Leone, a University student. These placed wreaths on monuments of Buxton, Zachary Macaulay, and Granville Sharp. All the wreaths bore the simple inscription, "From grateful Africans." Besides the persons already named the following were present: Sir Charles Dilke and Sir Brampton Gurdon—Members of Parliament, Colonel C. E. Macaulay and daughters, Bishop Ingham, Rev. Dr. Duckworth, Canon Beeching, Revs. John Philips and J. L. Hooppell, representatives of the society of Friends, Anti-Slavery Society, Congo Reform Association, the Church Missionary and the Wesleyan Missionary Societies, the Aborigines Protection Society, the African Training Institute, the African Society and the League of Universal Brotherhood. On the same day a telegram was received from the Ethiopian Progressive Association of Edinburgh offering best wishes for success. Late in the evening the Church Missionary Society transmitted a telegram received from Sierra Leone in which the people of that Colony requested that the Church Missionary Society should convey to the descendants of the liberators the expression of their greetings on the occasion of the Centenary the celebration of which was going on in that part of West Africa.

DYING

One of the fond hopes of the enemy is that we will kindly die off and leave the world white or at least that faded yellow which is by courtesy called white. The mainstay of this hope is expressed by Willcox in the Twelfth Census: the white death rate is 17 per thousand—the Negro 30, *ergo*, etc. But here comes one Rubinow, a Russian untainted by American mental colorations, and calls this in question; he says this death-rate is true but it is not racial but economic; we have here not a dying of black folk but a slaughter of the poor; in proof, he instances his own land. He says, "the condition, history and mode of life of the Russian peasant have many points of resemblance to the condition and life of the American Negro." In Russia, families owning no land had a death rate of 35 while those owning more than 135 acres each died at the rate of 20 per thousand. Others ranged between, according to poverty. "Text books of statistics never fail to indicate the enormous death-rate in Russia. Many explanations are given of it; and, (ours the italics) *were the Russians of a different hue the racial explanation would certainly claim a well-deserved prominence.*" The real cause of Negro excess in death-rate therefore, suggests Rubinow, is poverty.

RECORD

Sometime ago the Washington *Record* published a table of alleged Negro wealth which was false in every particular. The *Horizon* thinking the editor had made a mistake unwittingly, courteously called his attention to the fact that no such authentic compilation existed. Whereupon the editor blandly informs us that what the United States government has been unable to find out in 120 years of census work has been revealed to a benighted world by "W. H. Grimshaw" and that

> We hope this information will satisfy all persons concerned as well as justify us in our contention.

We commend to the heathen this evidence of a faith both childlike and bland.

EDITOR'S NOTE
†The reference is to T. Thomas Fortune. Du Bois published several articles in Fortune's New York newspaper, *The Globe* (later *The Freeman*) from 1883 to 1885.

6

The Over-Look

"Woe unto them that call evil good, and good evil; that put darkness for light, and light for darkness; that put bitter for sweet, and sweet for bitter!"

MAGAZINES

The South is silently boycotting the AMERICAN magazine: in Columbia, S. C., nearly the whole order lay in the book stalls while in Atlanta, it is almost impossible to buy a copy. Why? Read the June number.

Alexander Irvine is a Socialist and a Man. He heard the bitter cry of robbed and enslaved black workingmen and went to see. He writes in APPLETON'S for June.

The SATURDAY EVENING POST is continuing its role of yellow journalism by opening its pages continually to the Tillman-Dixon-Vardaman type of low demagoguery. This sort of thing pays and what else is the POST published for?

This is the list for the month:

My life in peonage—I., The situation as I found it. By Alexander Irvine, APPLETON, June.
Making an individual of the Indian. By J. M. Oskison. EVERYBODY'S, June.
The Negro in Southern city life. By Ray Stannard Baker, AMERICAN, June.
Uganda, Power of the Gospel in. Bishop Tucker. MISSIONARY REVIEW, June.
Liberia: the black republic. Sir Harry Johnston and U.S. Minister Lyon. NATIONAL GEOGRAPHIC MAGAZINE, May.
Yellow man's burden, The. Arthur Judson Brown. OUTLOOK, *April 20.*
Congo, American invasion of the. S. P. Verner. HARPER'S WEEKLY, May 4.
Negro problem, Governor Vardaman's idea of solving the. Harris Dickson. SATURDAY EVENING POST, April 27.

SATTERLEE

There comes a priest of the meek and lowly Jesus—a Servant of the Servant who said:
Blessed are the Meek,
  Blessed are the Poor,
    Blessed are the Merciful,
      Blessed are the Peace-makers,

From *The Horizon: A Journal of the Color Line* 1 (June 1907): 3–10.

Blessed are the Persecuted,
and chants to a waiting world this double-tongued litany:
Give black men a chance,
Because they are unable to take it.
Let them arise,
Since natural law keeps them down.
God speed their advance,
But men will jealously check it.
Up!
Down!
God pity the Episcopal church under such leadership. God succour Christianity amid such contradictions.

AFRICA

At the annual meeting of the Aborigines Protection Society of London the situation in South Africa is thus clearly portrayed:

> The position in South Africa is at the present time especially interesting. Cape Colony and Natal have had responsible government for several years. This great boon has now been accorded by His Majesty's Government to the Transvaal, and is on the point of being extended to the Orange River Colony. In these colonies the black or coloured population greatly outnumbers the white population; and a very grave responsibility is imposed on the white men residing therein. Being brought into immediate contact with these vast native populations, it is not, perhaps, unnatural that they should adopt a policy which tends to repress the development of the natives in all directions. It is an obvious truism that if education were imparted to these races it would be impossible to maintain them permanently in the subordinate position they now hold. Hence the colonists are very reluctant to extend education amongst them. That is, perhaps, the first difficulty with which we are confronted. Then there is the question of labour. The colonists expect to use the black population in developing the country for them. The result is that not only in these colonies, but everywhere in the world where white people—or, should we say, people of a higher state of civilization— are brought into contact with coloured populations, abuses prevail, the white races are demoralized, and the tendency to ill-treat the blacks becomes a very serious matter.
>
> But Great Britain is, after all, the mother country, responsible for her colonies. It is impossible for us, for our nation as a whole, to divest ourselves of the responsibilities we have incurred in dealing with the native races, and, in doing so, we have brought ourselves into serious conflict very often with our colonists in Natal. Natal is a colony in which the British population is less than 100,000—while the natives number about a million, and in addition there are about 100,000 British Indians who have settled there. Whatever may have been the reasons that first led to unrest in Natal, we know what has happened. The steps taken by the white population to destroy any feeling of independence which might have arisen among the Zulus and other coloured races fill a black page in the history of this country; and it is only typical of the difficulties with which we are always liable to be confronted in our South African dependencies.
>
> In the oldest colony in South Africa, however, we see a more satisfactory state of things. In Cape Colony the political rights of the coloured races have been officially recognized, and there is not much to complain of in the white man's relations with them; but Cape Colony at present stands alone in this matter, and the danger is very great that the policy which prevails in Natal, in the Transvaal, and in the Orange River Colony will influence Cape Colony, and deprive the coloured races in it of the privileges they now enjoy.

Efforts were made by the Society last year to procure for the natives some political rights in the Transvaal. But the Government considered that under the Treaty of Vereeniging this was impracticable, and if anything can now be done to enable the Transvaal natives ultimately to attain the standard which prevails in the Cape, it must be on the initiative of the white people of the Transvaal themselves. At the present moment the prospects of any move in this direction are very small.

The Aborigines Protection Society publishes the following works:

Blacks and Whites in South Africa. An account of the past treatment and present condition of South African natives under British and Boer control. Price 1 s.

Blacks and Whites in West Africa: An account of the past treatment and present condition of West African Natives under European influence and control. Price 1 s.

The Native Labour Question in the Transvaal: Extracts from the "Industrial Commission of Inquiry; Report and Proceedings." Published in Johannesburg in 1897. Price 1 s.

Egypt under British Control: I. The Conditions of British Supremacy; II. Reforming Efforts and Achievements; III. Failures and Omissions; IV. Present Opportunities and Obligations. Price 1 s.

Civilization in Congoland: A story of International Wrong doing. By H. R. Fox Bourne. Price 10 s 6d.

Buy them: Address Broadway Chambers, Westminster, S. W., London, England.

CARPENTERS

The Negro carpenters of New York are organizing for aggressive work. Says CHARITIES:

> Thirty-three Negro carpenters met last week at Public School No. 80, New York, to take joint action looking toward the improvement of opportunities for colored craftsmen in their trade. The meeting was indicative of a marked development in the Committee for Improving the Industrial Conditions of Negroes in New York. Probably no such meeting of Negro workmen had ever been held here before. They were addressed by the colored principal of a public school, by a Negro manufacturer and by a Negro union leader—one of the few men of his race who has stood high in the ranks of organized workers. Eight or nine union men were present and a total of sixty-two carpenters enrolled, in no small part men who because of difficulties and opposition in various quarters are today working outside their trades.

And led by a NIAGARA man.† Of course.

BROWNSVILLE

Whatever it did it made them think. It made us think. It will make the world think some day. Says the CHRISTIAN REGISTER, the leading Unitarian organ:

> One feature of the Brownsville discussion has impressed us peculiarly—the assumption of a conspiracy of silence on the part of the whole Negro troop at Brownsville. All have been held implicated in the offence, because none will give clue to the offenders. A few—say ten—committed the outrage: the remainder—say one hundred and sixty—with incriminating knowledge stubbornly withhold

it. Of course this may be possible; but whether credible, there may be two opinions. One hundred and sixty in possession of a grave secret, and it can be probed out of no one of them! One hundred and sixty incurring grave penalty from which a word would bring reprieve, and not one will speak it! We should stand in mute wonder in presence of constancy such as this. Such a secret in the possession of ten average white men would be extremely unsafe, and one hundred and sixty average Negroes! If to this length the Negroes will support one another, think what tribulations are yet before us in dealing with them!

They will never support one another to this length. A fiction, however, may call our attention to a fact, and this one may open our eyes to a tendency among the Negroes worth while to observe. There is no mistaking the fact that they are learning to cohere, to cooperate, to stand by one another; that a race interest is growing among them. This, to one who knew them in the sixties, implies significant change.

Now what has been the agent of this change? Education? In part undoubtedly. Knowledge and servility do not dwell comfortably together. The agent in chief, however, has been the hard treatment the Negro has experienced. Its aim has been to "teach him his place." It has put him on his feet, with the consciousness that he must work out his own destiny. The submissiveness and docility which gentleness might for a long time have perpetuated, severity has very largely obliterated. In like manner we may explain the race interest on which we have lingered. In bondage, this hardly existed. With freedom it was sure to come, but through the bitterness of the Negro's experience it has been immensely hastened.

BOOKS

Would you like to know of some good books for serious reading this summer? Well try:

Socialism: A summary and Interpretation of Socialist principles. By John Spargo.
War of the Classes. By Jack London.
Mass and Class: A Survey of Social Divisions. By Wm. J. Ghent.
The Social Unrest: Studies in labor and social movements. By John Graham Brooks.
The Labor Movement in America. By Richard T. Ely.
Democracy and Social Ethics. By Jane Addams.
The Menace of Privilege: A study of the dangers to the republic from the existence of a favored class. By Henry George, Jr.
Poverty. By Robert Hunter.
The Bitter Cry of the Children. By John Spargo.
The Care of Destitute, Neglected and Delinquent Children. By Homer Folks.
The Development of Thrift. By Mary Wilcox Brown.
Constructive and Preventive Philanthropy. By Joseph Lee.
The Battle with the Slums. By Jacob Riis.
People of the Abyss. By Jack London.
The Principles of Relief. By Dr. Edward T. Devine.
Newer Ideals of Peace. By Jane Addams.

Each of these Macmillan sells for the price of a four-in-hand tie, or all of them for an ostrich plume. And you can't afford them? Listen!

FULLER

A young Negro is rapidly becoming one of the best known of the younger Pathologists in America. In the AMERICAN JOURNAL OF INSANITY he published recently an article of sixty pages with bibliography and plates with certain results of his studies on insanity in Westborough Hospital, Mass. Silent, thorough, honest work is here *minus* the firework. And a NIAGARA man too.‡ Why not?

EDITOR'S NOTES
†This refers to William L. Bulkley, among the earliest Black principals of a New York City public school, who was later one of the founders of the N.A.A.C.P.

‡The reference is to Dr. Solomon Carter Fuller, the pioneer Black psychiatrist.

7

The Over-Look

THE MAGAZINES

This is the Month's menu:

Color Line, Following the: In the Black belt. Ray Stannard Baker. AMERICAN.
Japan's Ambition to Civilize Christendom. Harold Bolce. APPLETON.
Peonage, My life in—II., A week with the "Bull of the Woods." Alexander Irvine.
    APPLETON.
Maori Girls, The Training of. MISSIONARY REVIEW.
Guiana Wilderness, The. Angelo Heilprin. NATIONAL GEOGRAPHIC MAGAZINE, June.
Negro Soldier, The, in Peace and War. Stephen Bonsal. NORTH AMERICAN, June 7.
Negro, Soul of the. LIVING AGE, June 1.
Congo Free State, King Leopold and the. Richard Harding Davis. COLLIER, June 15.
Kongo Question, King Leopold's Views on the. M. Van Holsen. INDEPENDENT, May 23.
Japanese in America. John Foord. OUTLOOK, May 18.
Negro, Progress of the. Booker T. Washington. INDEPENDENT, June 13.
Subject Races, The Rights of. Henry W. Nevinson. LIVING AGE, June 8.

From *The Horizon: A Journal of the Color Line* 2 (July 1907): 3.

24

8

The Over-Look

THE MAGAZINES

The most of the relatively few articles relating to "us" in their magazines are continuations. The articles include:

Negro's Up Hill Climb, A—conclusion. Robert Russa Moton. WORLD'S WORK.
Color Line, Following the. White Man and Negro in the black belt. Ray Stannard Baker. AMERICAN.
Peonage, My Life in—III. The kidnapping of "Punk." Alexander Irvine. APPLETON.
Race Question, The, in the 46th State. L. J. Abbott. INDEPENDENT, (July 25th.)
Race Problem, The. Maud Meredith. TOMORROW (Chicago.)

The last named magazine is one of the "Special" class, "for people who think" it says. It is rather unconventional, and socialistic. Speaks of "us" often and is stiffly for us, always.

We should have mentioned last month, *The Dred Scott case,* under the heading, "Decisive Battles of Law," by Frederick Trevor Hill, in HARPER's Magazine for July. A fine article which shows how an apparently trivial case was made the vehicle of a great political maneuver by the slave power. And incidentally it shows how important it is that legal cases involving our rights be carefully watched and adequately defended.

A REBUKE

The New York *Independent* in its issue of July 18th hands Bishop Satterlee this:

> Let us say to Bishop Satterlee that he is as ignorant of the Negroes as he confesses he was, until lately, of the Methodists. The colored people of America are not concerned about social recognition, only about their equal personal rights. They do not admit that they are intellectually or physically inferior to any other race; they are only a little later getting started. They have an ambition, a reasonable one, which we will do our best to support, that in intelligence, culture, wealth and genius they may prove themselves equal to the best the world has yet produced. We expect to see men of that blood occupying the highest positions in this country, all conceited and arrogant Caucasian or Anglo-Saxon assumption to the contrary notwithstanding. We want to see it; it is decently Christian to desire it.

And what is Fame? the meanest have their day, The Greatest can but blaze and pass away.

—Pope—Horace.

From *The Horizon: A Journal of the Color Line* 2 (August 1907): 3–4.

9

The Over-Look

"There is a poor blind Samson in this land
Shorn of his strength and bound in bonds of steel
Who may in some grim revel, raise his hand
And shake the pillars of this common-weal
Till the vast Temple of our liberties
A shapeless mass of rubbish lies."

—Longfellow

THE MAGAZINES

They are giving us our summer vacation this month. You see there are other "Niggers" to have their innings—those impudent Japanese in British Columbia and Mexico, and the nasty East Indians, not to mention Jews and Italians and other trash. What does God mean by allowing such things to live when His own children want the earth and the fulness thereof?

The Negro Situation, by W.J. Northen, also—
A Negro College Town, by Booker T. Washington. WORLD'S WORK.
Negro Education, by Leroy Percy. OUTLOOK, August 3.

God rest St. Gaudens. I never pass the Shaw Memorial without feeling more of a man than before.†

NIAGARA

We have passed the Third Mile Stone. The first was Derision—O how cheerily they laughed in sleeve and apron: the second was Misrepresentation—we were agitators, sore-heads, personal enemies, and much else of the like. This year it was Disruption—we could not stand, our doom was written in the stars. And yet withal we have grown and we have done things, not many but some:

1. We own the celebrated steel-engraved plate of John Brown
by Sartain.
2. We have fought and won the Pope "Jim Crow" case.
3. We have helped in defending the Soldiers.
4. We have enrolled 400 members in 35 states.

From *The Horizon: A Journal of the Color Line* 2 (September 1907): 3–6, 8–10.

5. We have kept up the campaign of agitation for Negro rights until the country is awakening to the fact that all colored men are not cowards, beggars or compromisers.

We have plans in abundance for the future and these are our words today:

Address

For the third time the Niagara Movement in its annual meeting appeals to the world and to America. This has been a year of wrong and discrimination. There sits today in the governor's chair of a sovereign Southern commonwealth a man stained with the blood of innocent black workingmen, who fell in the Atlanta massacre, and whose unavenged death cries to God for justice. What answer does Georgia return? The fraudulent disfranchisement of her citizens, and with the echo of her fell attack on Democracy sounds the eager voices of a great tribunal dedicated to industrial freedom, which has in unseemly haste scurried to uphold social slavery and the vicious and nasty Jim-Crow car. And why not? Has not the man in the White House set them brave example by bowing before the brown and armed dignity of Japan, and swaggering roughshod over the helpless black regiment whose bravery made him famous? With such example, why should not the lawless and vicious of the land take courage? Why should not the less civilized parts of our country follow this lead and spread the mockery of the Republican government in the South? But we will not follow. We are Americans. We believe in this land. We cannot silent see it false to its great ideals. We call for repentance, reparation, reconsecration to the ideals of Washington, Jefferson and our own Hamilton. We demand freedom from labor peonage. We demand a free and fair ballot. We demand the denial of national representation to the states who deny the rights of citizens. We demand federal legislation forbidding exclusion of any persons from interstate cars on account of race or color. We ask common school training for every child if necessary at national expense. We demand full exoneration and re-instatement of our shamefully libeled soldiers, and finally, in God's name, we ask justice, and not only do we ask and pray, but we back our prayer by deeds. We call on the 500,000 free black voters of the North. Use your ballots to defeat Theodore Roosevelt, William Taft, or any man named by the present political dictatorship. Better vote for avowed enemies than for false friends. But, better still, vote with the white laboring classes, remembering that the cause of labor is the cause of black men, and the black man's cause is labor's own.

We are not discouraged. We thank God for life and health and property, for shade and shine and above all for the opportunity in the twentieth century of Jesus Christ to fight the battle of humanity in the very van of His army. Help us, brothers, for the victory which lingers, must and shall prevail.

CHAINS

A recent writer—J.H. Collins—in a western paper says:

> While in London, in 1905, I obtained interesting information relating to the anti-slavery sentiment in England three-quarters of a century ago. One Sunday evening I went to the old Kingsgate Baptist Church, just off Southampton Row, near Dickens' "Old Curiosity Shop," and in the vicinity of the abode of the

original "Sary Gamp." At the close of the service an official of the church announced that, as there were a number of visitors present who would probably be interested to learn something of the history of this old church, all who desired to do so were invited to remain after the congregation was dismissed.

Among other matters of interest he told this story: Rev. William Knibb was a member of this church during the latter half of the nineteenth century. He went as a missionary to Jamaica, and, while preaching the gospel there, came in contact with the slave system and was deeply and profoundly stirred on account of the evils connected with it. He took a strong stand against slavery and on account of his attitude upon this question he was compelled to leave. He returned to England and became one of the leaders of a campaign against slavery in the colonies which did not cease until laws were enacted abolishing slavery in all English colonies.

When the appointed time arrived for the law to go into effect in Jamaica, Rev. Knibb was there to witness the liberation of the slaves. He found a Negro man in chains whom he prevailed upon to accompany him to England wearing the chains he had worn as a slave. Upon their arrival at London a great meeting was called at this church to celebrate the freedom of slaves in Jamaica. In the presence of the large concourse of people assembled, this slave in chains was seated on the platform and a blacksmith cut from his ankles the manacles he had worn so long. In commemoration of the freedom of the slaves and the part this church had taken in bringing about this event, a sum of money was raised and a school founded. When the corner-stone was laid these chains were placed within it.

NEGLECTED DUTY

This is history. May it not also be prophecy?

Arsenius was the tutor of Arcadius and Honorius, the sons of Emperor Theodosius, having the responsibility of their education. He lived in great splendor at the court of the emperor in Constantinople, neglecting his great duty to the future emperors. Not a noble lesson did he impress upon his pupils.

As emperor, Arcadius was characterized by utter incompetence and weakness, and Honorius by his frivolity, devoting his attention to poultry breeding instead of governing his empire.

Their tutor fled to the desert to escape, if possible, all reminders of his neglected duty. The hermits hailed him as the father of the emperors. It was the keenest sarcasm but well deserved. He fled from them to seek entire solitude in the wildest waste. There in absolute silence and constant remorse, he spent the long years. Men visited his cave, but could never induce him to speak. He wept until the lashes were worn from his eyelids, hoping by his austerities to atone for his sins of omission which had degraded the empire. Thus he continued till his death.—*Foster.*

————

She walketh veiled and sleeping,
    For she knoweth not her power;
She obeyeth but the pleading
Of her heart, and the high leading
    Of her soul unto this hour.
Slow advancing, halting, creeping,
    Comes the Woman to the hour!—
She walketh veiled and sleeping,
    For she knoweth not her power.
                    —Charlotte Gibman.

EDITOR'S NOTE
†Augustus Saint-Gaudens, a famous American sculptor, created a figure of Robert Gould Shaw which stands in the
Boston Commons. Shaw, the Abolitionist, became a Colonel
in the Civil War and commanded the Black 54th Massachusetts Infantry; he was killed in the Fort Wagner, S.C.,
assault in 1865.

10

The Over-Look

"And can it be that the intensive fire that
    made them men,—
Not trees, nor creeping beasts, nor stones,
    nor stars,—
And gave identity to every soul,
Making it individual and alone
Among the myriads; and can it be
That when the mortal framework failed,—
    that fire
Which flamed in separate and lonely life,
These souls, slipped out of being and were lost,
Eternally extinguished and cast out?"
           R. W. Gilder in the ATLANTIC.

THE MAGAZINES

During October we may read Salvini's interpretation of "Othello" in PUTNAM'S, and Washington on, "The Negro of Today." In the POLITICAL SCIENCE QUARTERLY, Phillips writes of slave labor, while the METROPOLITAN lets a certain Dimock talk of "The South and its Problems." In the weeklies, Georgia is discussed in the INDEPENDENT (Aug. 22) and the OUTLOOK (Aug. 31, Sept. 14), and CHARITIES has two articles: on the Hampton Conference (Aug. 24) and the "Negro Problem in Washington" (Sept. 14).

THE FOREIGN VIEW

How can race prejudice be modified?

"In the history of the world it has practically come about to a vast extent by interbreeding and mixture of races. And though the idea of this method may be scouted as out of the range of practical consideration or influence in connection with modern colour problems, and though I should admit that it may tend to diminish in importance as compared with direct mental influences, yet I consider that the tendency of opinion and sentiment at the present in the ascendant is unduly to undervalue its real importance, and I propose to give reasons for thinking that where it takes place that it is advantageous. We should at least give full credit to its possibilities before passing to consider other methods of fusion.

"The question of the relations between black and white is obscured by a mass of prejudice and ignorance and blindness, proportional to the isolating difference in their evolved constitutions. Those barriers are not different in kind or in strength from those which once separated neighbouring European tribes. What has happened as between these we can trace and recognize, and this recognition will help us to approach the contemporary problem."
           Olivier in "White Capital
           and Colored Labor" (English).

From *The Horizon: A Journal of the Color Line* 2 (October 1907): 3–10.

"Professor Lamprecht has the usual kind word for American architecture, but considers the ragtime melodies of the Negroes to be the only truly spontaneous and indigenous form of American art. It is the duty of every American musician to have these collected and examined."

Atlantic on Karl Lamprecht's
"Americana" (German).

"Mr. Wells's sense of pity in the problem of the Negro is moved mainly by what he calls the 'tainted whites.' He is amazed, as I think every non-American must be, at the way in which a few drops of Negro blood is held to outweigh a ninety per cent infusion of the best white blood in the country. He thinks it does not say much for the American's faith in his own racial prepotency."

Atlantic on H. G. Wells "The
Future in America" (English).

"At the present time it is a vain task to seek distinctive characteristics among certain products of Negroes crossed with Whites. Dr. Pearce Kintzing, who devoted several years of his life to the study of this question, mentions the same fact in American Medicine (July 1904).

"He tells how he can no longer find means of distinguishing mixed blood from white blood, except in American novels. In real life everything deceives us, including the colour of the nails, which, according to certain lady novelists of the South, is so infallible. In order to dissipate all illusions, Dr. Kintzing for three years submitted to close examination, 500 patients from among the Whites and Blacks. The students were called to decide as to the origin of the subject, who was completely covered except the nails. But the errors were so obvious and so frequent that Dr. Kintzing finally rejected the nails as a characteristic sign. Other significant traits deceive us in like manner. The same author quotes cases of coloured children in the hospital who were entered as whites.

"The persecution and injustice of the Whites, however, continue their work. Worried and despised, the 'Blacks', including even those who have ceased to be such, become more and more united, and constitute a kind of State within a State. The humiliations suffered by them all in common hasten this unifying process. It may be said that the Negroes are being driven back upon themselves, while the present miseries of their existence are impeding the process of their moral and intellectual liberation.

"Everything in the meantime permits us to believe that this is an arrest of a somewhat sentimental nature. The Negroes, far from being discouraged, resume their efforts, and are working valiantly for the emancipation of their thought and their persons.

"The school of sorrow is the best of schools. It has been proved by nearly all people (and one observes the same phenomenon among individuals regarded singly) that adversity and privation only quicken and develop the intellectual faculties and ameliorate the moral life. The Negroes, always in the school of misfortune, become more moral and more enlightened, more rich and more independent. Their physiological progress, to use anthropological language, being aided by their intellectual progress, an impartial observer can already foresee the time, not too far distant, when the two hostile races shall arrive at understanding and unity."

Finot: "Race Prejudice" (French).

TWO LETTERS

A Bishop of the Episcopal Church writes me:

"Naturally as a Bishop I am somewhat perplexed by the question which is certain to come before us at the General Convention soon to meet at Richmond. Personally I can think of no practical difficulty with which I could not deal were I

a Bishop in a Southern State. . . . . . I have no race prejudice. As far as I am concerned I am perfectly willing to accept upon terms of absolute equality any man who is my moral and intellectual peer. . . . . . My brethren in the episcopate, however, feel differently. Many of the Negro clergy advocate for this reason and for others a policy which I should consider would be unwise. . . . . . You evidently feel very strongly as to the theory but in view of the irritation felt by the colored people with existing conditions and the clamorous demands from the Negro clergy for a Bishop of their own race, what would you advise as a wise policy?"
To this I replied:

"I think that the most practical thing that the Episcopal Convention would do with regard to the Negro in the Church would be to affirm solemnly the essential equality of all members of the Church, insist upon their representation in all assemblies, and endeavor to the best of its ability and power to have the present regulations of the Church carried out without regard to race or color. I do not think the time has yet come when it is necessary for the Church to surrender to Colorphobia, and I sincerely hope that you will give your vote and voice to the resistance of any such thing. I should regard the election of a distinct Bishop for Negroes as being unwise and uncalled for at present. Of course, as I have said in my book, if the Church can not stand up to its profession, if it can not stand today for Christian brotherhood even in the modified sense in which this exists among White Churchmen, then, I and my fellows will soon be compelled to receive some distinct and different treatment. But I am not personally ready to acknowledge at this time the necessity of such a step and I shall be very sorry to see any such action taken."

NEWS FROM ALABAMA

"Dear Sir: Yours received. You ask me of the man that was lynched. He was Pettigrew, and was lynched without being allowed five minutes to tell the facts or to prove himself innocent. With 67 White men about him, well armed, he was shot to death. The last words I heard him say, were: 'God knows I did not do it'. Since then two white men were charged with being concerned in the crime. After he was killed he was dragged on the ground with his feet tied behind a buggy to a place a mile out of town. He was 26 years old and did not fear any white man. Don't care what number of letters you get this is the whole truth. If you want any particulars send a registered letter. We can't tell what we want to in this town."

(Signed) . . . .

This is commended to the editor of the OUTLOOK as a basis for an editorial on "the best people of the South."

EGYPT

"Commencing with Herodotus, whose statements are more weighty, as they are the result of personal observation, we find that historian asserting the Egyptian origin of the people of Colchis and supporting his assertion by the argument that they were 'black in complexion and woolly haired.' Copying the Halicarnassian in his fourth Pythian ode, Pindar also described the Colchians as being black. And Herodotus in another passage, when relating the fable of the Dodonian Oracle, again alludes to the swarthy colour of the Egyptians, 'as if it were exceedingly dark, and even black.' Further, in his supplices, Æschylus, mentioning the crew of an Egyptian bark that was seen from the shore, alludes to the person who espied it as having arrived at the conclusion that its members were Egyptians, on account of their black complexion.

> 'The sailors too I marked
> Conspicuous in white robes their sable limbs.'

"Now, from all that has been said in connection with the question as to 'who were the Ancient Egyptians?' the answer, it will be seen, is discernible in the three following directions: The philological, the physical, and the historical.

"In the philological direction we have noticed that the wide unbridged unbridgeable difference between the Egyptian tongue and the Semitic or Aramæan, on the one hand, and the Indo-European, on the other hand, excludes the old Egyptian nation from these races; while the complete likeness of its language to the numerous dialects of the African tribes and nations mark its affinity to the Hamitic race.

"In the physical direction we have observed that, whereas, on the ground of complexion, the fairer section of the Egyptians, as represented on their monuments, in their paintings, etc., may be classed with either the Indo-European, Semitic, or the Hamitic race, as regards the hair of the head and the contour of the face, they were decidedly Hamitic. And among certain Negro tribes, now inhabiting the African continent—as I shall show in the next chapter—not only do we find the 'lighter' and 'darker' shades of colour which were present among the Egyptians but these shades are exhibited in the same proportion as they appeared among the Egyptians; so that the physical identity between the Ancient Egyptians and the Negro race is completely established.

"Lastly, in the historical direction, while we have, on the one hand, modern authorities, such as Heeren and Featherman, Nott and Gliddon, arguing against the Negro origin of the Egyptians, on the other we have authorities, such as Volney, Prichard, and Rollins arguing in favour of the Negro origin. And on proceeding to the testimony of ancient witnesses, that is to say those who had had personal knowledge of the Egyptians, such, for instance, as Herodotus, who had himself travelled in Egypt, we find the testimony of these witnesses to be both unanimous and unequivocal in the declaration that the Egyptians were blacks, in fact that they were Negroes. Thus, by the harmony of this powerful triplex of proofs, I am finally compelled to pronounce in the favour of the Negro origin of the Egyptians."

Scholes, "Glimpse of the Ages," (1905).†

EDITOR'S NOTE
†The reference is to the first volume of a two-volume work by Theophilus E. S. Scholes: *Glimpses of the Ages; or, The "Superior" and "Inferior" Races, So-called, Discussed in the Light of Science and History,* London, J. Long, 1905–1908.

11

The Over-Look

"Though Justice against Fate complain,
And plead the ancient Rights in vain—
But those do hold or break
As men are strong or weak."

THE MAGAZINES FOR NOVEMBER

Meta Vaux Warrick, Sculptor, W. T. O'Donnell. WORLD TODAY.
The Negro and the South, John Sharp Williams. METROPOLITAN.
French in North Africa, C. W. Furlong. WORLD'S WORK.
Liberia, Bishop I. B. Scott. INDEPENDENT (Sept. 26).
Menelik of Abyssinia, S. Cortesi. INDEPENDENT (Oct. 10).
White Canada, R. Brown. HARPER'S WEEKLY (Oct. 5.).
A Kentucky Negro Mission, L. J. Speed. CHARITIES (Sept. 21).
The Negro Building at Jamestown, H. A. Tucker. CHARITIES (Sept. 21).

BOOKS

Reminiscences of Carl Schurz. 2 Vol. McClure. $6.00
Autobiography: Oliver Otis Howard. 2 Vol. Baker & Taylor. $5.00
Alexander Dumas: My Memoirs. 6 Vol. Macmillan, $1.75.
John Greenleaf Whittier by Bliss Perry. Houghton, 75 cents.
Mam' Linda by W. N. Harben. Harper's. $1.50.

Persons able to beg or borrow six dollars and a half should buy General Howard's reminiscences, and Harben's "Mam' Linda." The latter is the fairest bit of race problem fiction which a native Southerner has written for many a year. Harben is a white Georgian. He knows, as most white southerners do, two types of Negro: the faithful old freed-man and the careless young vagabond. Differing from most white southerners however, he has set himself the task of asking something more than monuments and ropes for these: he asks Justice. Good! Now for the next step, let him and his realize the independent, self-assertive, thrifty black men who demand their rights as American citizens, not because of their color, but because of their manhood. Howard? But why should I speak to you of the founder of Howard University and the head of the Freedmen's Bureau? His book should be in every Negro's home. The other two also are worth HORIZON-room.

From *The Horizon: A Journal of the Color Line* 2 (November 1907): 1–7.

SELECTIONS FROM THE HORIZON   35

BURTON

Let us pray God that the defeat of Burton, of Cleveland, Ohio, but fore-runs the overthrow of the whole Roosevelt-Taft machine, which he represented. You can insult ten million people and shoot bears with their enemies, but you cannot bank on the votes of such of them as have backbones. The Negro who votes for Theodore Roosevelt or any of his ilk is worse than a traitor to his race—he is a fool.

12

The Over-Look

I dimly guess what Time in mists confounds:
Yet ever and anon a trumpet sounds
From the hid battlements of eternity:
These shaken mists a space unsettle, then
Round the half-glimpsed turrets slowly wash again;
    But not ere Him who summoneth
    I first have seen, enwound
With glooming robes purpureal, cypress crowned;
His name I know, and what his trumpet saith.
—Thompson.

THE CHRISTMAS MAGAZINES

Whittier,† Putnam's, Book News Monthly, Atlantic, Lippincott's.
Hindu Immigrants in America, E. M. Wherry, Missionary Review.
Yellow Peril, The Real, Hugh H. Lusk. North American, (Nov.).
So. African Native Situation, J. DuPlessis. Missionary Review.
Christmas in old Virginia, Booker T. Washington. Suburban Life.
Negro Building and Exhibit at Jamestown Exposition, William Hayes Ward. Independent, (Nov. 14.)
Negro, The, and Justice, Independent, (Oct. 17.)
Southern Election Registrar, Power of the, Thomas Jesse Jones. Outlook, (Nov. 9.)
$25,000, Raising, in 26 Days, Booker T. Washington. Independent, (Nov. 7.)

A BOOK

Eaton: *Grant, Lincoln, and the Freedmen;* Longmans, 1907. $2.00

"My second wish was to preserve, in a form available to the general reader, a record of the efforts made by the Union Army to succor the Negro during the progress of the war, and to secure justice to him and to the communities in which he found himself. Here, again, no attempt has been made to give a history of this work in any adequate or general sense. Although I have the keenest recognition of the labors of other men who were detailed to special service among the contrabands and freedmen, I have been obliged to refer only sparingly to their efforts. I have confined myself to presenting as faithfully as I might, a record of the work for the Negro in the Mississippi Valley, where I acted as Superintendent of Freedmen for the Department of the Tennessee and the State

From *The Horizon: A Journal of the Color Line* 2 (December 1907): 1–8.

of Arkansas, under the direct authority of General Grant—and later of the War department—and in more or less close personal touch with President Lincoln.

"The superintendency established by the Union over the welfare of the Negro during the height of the conflict was one of the most important efforts made by our Government to meet the threatening race problem which was then presented unequivocally to the Nation, and which is still one of the great issues our country has to face. Under that supervision the Negro's status changed from that of slave to freedman, and the record of the transformation should at least be available to all who have an interest in the Negro question as it confronts us today. Unfortunately no one of the superintendents intrusted with this work before the establishment of the Freedmen's Bureau has given us any history of it save what may be drawn from the somewhat inaccessible official reports. Hence the literature of the subject is inadequate. Yet the Negro can never be understood or our relation to him determined until all the elements in his history are recognized. It is in the hope, then, of preserving data which are in danger of being wholly overlooked that these personal recollections are offered."

From the Preface.

AN ESSAY BY A SOUTHERN WHITE BOY

The Negro is a free people and ought to be, What would the white man do without the Negro? Many white men have got rich off the Negro and nothing but the Negro.

The white men hire the Negro to work for them and if the work does not suit them, they will not pay the Negro. What did the white man bring the Negro over here for if he did not want them. It is said that the white men are trying to run the Negro out of the South; instead of running the Negro out how come that the white men don't get out themselves. The Negro has as much right to the South as the white men have. The white men talk about the Negro so much I want them to show me a Negro. Nearly every Negro in the United States is half bred. The Negro works hard for his money and when he goes to spend it, the white men get two-thirds more than the stuff is worth. The white men think that the Negro has no rights at all. When the Northern people were trying to free the Negro, the Negro staid at home and took care of the white men's families. Some white men think that they are too good to work, but when the Negro is gone he will have it to do. If the white men kill the Negro it is all right, but if the Negro kills the white man they have him peoned. If the Negro gets in a tight place the white man will not help him out, but when the white man gets in trouble, the Negro is ready to help him out.

Charles Manning,

(eleven years old; Son of J. C. Manning, of Alabama).

A HERO

John B. Hill, of Atlanta, coachman of Willis Ragan, of 574 Peachtree street, was the first Negro to secure recognition at the hands of the Carnegie award committee, being given a Carnegie medal and $500 to reimburse him for injuries received in making the rescue for which he was decorated.

Months ago the carriages of Henry Inman and J. E. Hunnicutt collided and two runaways resulted. As the Hunnicutt vehicle, in which were seated a nurse and two little boys, was carried in wild flight down Peachtree street, the predicament of the occupants was noted by John Hill, who leaped a fence and stopped the buggy after being thrown down and dragged for some distance before accomplishing his purpose.

He had just recovered from an operation, and the injuries received in stopping the runaway put him in bed again for several weeks.—*Atlanta Constitution.*

REPORT

A Native Affairs Commission in South Africa made several recommendations—

"Foremost among them is the proposal that only those who are racially, and of full consanguinity, connected with some African tribe following the tribal system, accepting polygamy and the rule of a chief, should be placed under native law. It is added:

'This proposition is intended to be far-reaching in its effects, as it not only affords a clearer exposition of the term than any others which have been attempted, but it is expressly designed to release that large body of intelligent and respectable persons known as "half-castes" from the operation of this law, and from which they have been desirous of freeing themselves for years. As a rule they are monogamists, and conform their lives to civilized usages, and their aspirations, notwithstanding many drawbacks, are impressively towards the legal position of their "white father," objecting to being thrust down to the level of their "black mother." . . .

'Condemned by the Europeans and distrusted by the native, moral duty and political expediency alike demand that the representations which appear in evidence should be generously entertained. To give effect to this recommendation would be a simple, yet skilful, diplomatic move, and it would not hinder the community if they were also freed from the disabilities regarding the use of liquor and fire-arms. It is strongly urged that the time has come when all who attune their lives according to those of the dominant race should live under the same laws and exercise the same privileges. In laws imposing disabilities the classes intended to be brought within their operation should be specifically named without attempting therein to define the term "native." ' "

CLAY

An unwritten page in the history of American politics came to light in the city hall today, when Mrs. Mary Hunter (colored) 95 years old, and an ex-slave, gave her version of the failure of Henry Clay to be elected to the presidency of the United States in 1832. Mrs. Hunter was a slave and was at the famous banquet given by the state of North Carolina to Henry Clay at Asheville. Miles of tables were spread through the trees and no greater enthusiasm was ever shown over a political event than was displayed there. Nearly all the prominent of the South were there and the name of Clay was on every tongue. His election seemed assured until a cloud of scandal crossed the horizon. Henry Clay fell in love with a beautiful octoroon, who had been freed by her master in North Carolina. The secret was exposed a few days after the banquet, says Mrs. Hunter, and for many weeks the beautiful girl was the object of all gossip in that part of the country. "My mother knew the girl well," said Mrs. Hunter, "and the talk started caused her to disappear. No one ever heard of her after that."

—Minneapolis Journal

ADVERTISEMENT OF "ST. NICHOLAS STORIES"

"A glance at this book will show us that a different atmosphere envelops the Sunny South . . . Stories of Negro children and alligators bring up other characteristic features."

EDITOR'S NOTE
†1907 marked the centennial of the birth of John Greenleaf
Whittier, "the slave's poet." This explains the rash of essays
on him as well as the appearance of the Bliss Perry biography
noted by Du Bois under "Books" the previous November.

13

The Over-Look

The stars are in my pulses,—
And white the wind-swept snow!
Strike spur and Slacken bridle;
We'll ride forever so!

Hinchman.

1907

Debit	Credit
Brownsville	Peonage trials
Maryland election	Emancipation of Fortune
Jeff Davis	Foraker
The Tyler sop	Kentucky election
South Africa	Cleveland election
Congo	Baker's magazine articles
Oklahoma	Exit Vardaman
The *Voice*	Exit Dixon
The *Conservator*	Potter, Ferguson and Episcopalians
The *Age* ($9,500)	Jeanes Fund
Jamestown	Liberia's boundary
	Locke at Oxford
	Pope-Niagara case
	Braithwaite
	Mam' Linda
	Y. M. C. A. in D. C.

MAGAZINE ARTICLES OF 1907

Wells, *Race Prejudice*, INDEPENDENT, Feb. 14.
Parke, *Story of Congo*. EVERYBODY'S, Jan., etc.
Gladden. AMERICAN, Jan.
Moton, *Autobiography*. WORLD'S WORK, April, May, etc.
Baker, *Following the Color Line*. AMERICAN, April, May, etc.
Irvine, *Peonage*. APPLETON, June, July, etc.
Johnston and Lyon, *Liberia*. NATIONAL GEOGRAPHIC MAGAZINE, May.
O'Donnell, *Meta Warrick*. WORLD TODAY, Nov.

From *The Horizon: A Journal of the Color Line* 3 (January 1908): 1–5, 6–8.

BOOKS OF 1907

Finot: *Race Prejudice.*
Olivier: *White Capital and Coloured Labor.*
Eaton: *Grant, Lincoln and the Freedmen.*
Howard: *Autobiography.*

NEW YEAR

A Happy New Year means first, *Health.* Why not have it? It costs so little to keep, and even lost it may be regained in so many cases without absolute bankruptcy. Why not put down *Health* first then? Next, *Work*—something worth doing. Day after day of tired sinews and brain, in something that pays: pays in contentment, pays in happiness, and—if no more—pays in cash. Next, *More Work*—something *else* to do, and something different, yet something that tells: brain-work, if you work with your hands—hand-work, if you work with your brains; and yet and always something worth while. Next, *Love.* Nothing maudlin, but human affection arising from human acquaintance: know some Soul—help it, and be helped by it. Then know another soul. Don't be afraid: your sympathy won't give out, for bankruptcy in human affections, like that in money matters, is hastened rather than averted by hoarding. Finally, *Air.* Get outdoors; take in a sunset or two—watch the cloud masses, which you haven't seen in so long, and listen to a bird song. All this, and the HORIZON promises you a Happy New Year.

BOOKS AND PAPERS

Now comes the season when we calculate how much we dare give to the year's feeding of our souls. We need a daily paper, of course—more's the pity—and then a race paper, a weekly digester, a monthly picture-gallery, and an Encourager. As to the daily, the HORIZON will not presume to suggest, nor can we hope to convert you to our favorite race weekly, (which, some spell with an A); but we do suggest as a "digester" the *Independent,* as a monthly the *American* (wobbly, but trying hard) and as an Encourager—why—US. Then add, possibly: *Charities,* (weekly) New York, $2.00; *African Mail,* (weekly) Liverpool, $5.00. Finally, for books, ten dollars would be a modest sum for such as read and write—others, five.

PEONAGE†

Nothing is more easy than to miss the favorable things that are happening for us, because of the news and lack of news in the newspapers. Who, for instance, among us is aware that twelve southern white men have, in the last year or two, been convicted of peonage, and that several of them are actually basking in the penitentiary this moment? And this too in spite of the complacency and lying that whispers: All is well in the South. Nor is this due to any virtues of Theodore the Perfect; rather it is due to the persistent prodding of the Italian and Grecian ministers, which has set the Government hunting after slave-holders in the South, and incidentally it has emancipated a few Negroes. To be sure as yet only the edges have been touched: that great stronghold of slavery—the Mississippi delta, southern Arkansas, and northern Louisiana—still lies unentered, and we may trust Senatorial courtesy to keep it so as long as we continue to have a Southern president. Do you remember the hubbub about Judge Swayne in Florida, last year? Swayne was convicting slave-holders; the idea! Impeachment was threatened; then there is a brave little woman in Washington—how the Congressmen denounce her; meantime she is sending some of their most prominent constituents to jail. Whom the gods would destroy—.

HUBERT

The lecture recently delivered by M. Luciene Hubert before the Society of Arts in London is one that ought to be read by everyone—be he merchant or administrator—who is associated or interested in West Africa, for M. Hubert speaks to the point with a conciseness and directness that is refreshing, and there is many a good practical lesson to be learnt from what he says. Although conceding, and conceding handsomely, to England all that is her due as being the first and foremost Colonial Power with respect to material resources, as being, too, the initiator of the policy which should be followed in regard to native races, M. Hubert boldly admits France has followed the English example too slavishly. England it is true, he says, has respected the customs and the habits of the natives, and enabled them to live in comfort under the benefits of English civilization. But France must go still further. It was not sufficient that they should protect the natives of their own colonies—they must assist them. *They must not only give them liberty, they must also create in them the idea of progress. They must teach them not only to respect their own interests, but the interests of others.* To do this, M. Hubert laid great and special emphasis on the need for co-operation among the White peoples in the treatment of native races; and he might well have added, co-operation between governors and governed. These are brave and noble words, and the principles and policy they inculcate are of the very highest order, while the ideal aimed at comes within the scope of that broad humanitarianism that tends towards the moral elevation of the human race—*African Mail.*

WIDGEON

The life story of John W. Widgeon, the colored porter of the Maryland Academy of Sciences, is almost as remarkable as that of Jas. (?) Banneker,‡ the famous negro astronomer of early nineteenth century days.

Born in slavery on a Virginia plantation, Widgeon is now a man of exact and varied scientific knowledge. It would not be hyperbole to call him a scientist, though the term is so loosely applied ordinarily as to have little force. He does all of the collecting of the Maryland Academy of Sciences and has been its representative many times in foreign countries on expeditions to gather objects of scientific interest.

His discoveries have often contributed new knowledge to science. Only this year he made three discoveries in the State of Maryland that will be given a prominent place in the annual report of the institution by which he is employed.

Widgeon was born in Northampton county, Virginia, before the war. He has been a house boy, a butcher, photographer's assistant, a photographer and a chemist.

One of the most noteworthy feats that he ever accomplished was the ascent of Blue Mountain Peak, in Jamaica, and the taking of photographs from the summit. Blue Mountain Peak is more than 7,000 feet high, and it is rarely ascended. There are few photographs taken from the top of it in existence. There can be little doubt that the ones that Widgeon got are the best ever made.

To get to the top of the mountain Widgeon had to wade through streams of mud neck high and had to climb treacherous, slimy banks at an angle of almost 90 degrees. He started at 9 in the morning to make the climb and did not reach the end of his journey until 10:30 at night. The trip up the mountain side covered a distance of more than 19 miles. The mountain itself is about a mile and a quarter high.

Very recently Widgeon went to Jamaica and made a large collection of corals. This collection is one of the chief exhibits in the Academy of Sciences now. There was only one diver of experience in the island of Jamaica, so Widgeon had to learn diving himself to get the coral he wanted.

"Have I an invaluable colored man?" repeated Dr. Philip R. Uhler, president of the academy, resentfully not liking the way in which the question had been put.

"Why, he is more than a 'man.' That man is a scientist. I don't know what we would do without him."—Baltimore Sun.

EDITOR'S NOTES

†For elucidation of the matters discussed here and the actions of Judge Charles Swayne, see: Daniel, Pete, *The Shadow of Slavery: Peonage in the South, 1901–1969*. (Urbana: University of Illinois Press, 1972): 3–18.

‡It is of some interest that a writer for the Baltimore *Sun* did not know the name of Benjamin Banneker (1731–1806), the celebrated self-taught Black mathematician and astronomer from Maryland.

14

The Over-Look

If you would lift me, you must be on higher ground. If you would liberate me, you must be free. If you would correct my false view of facts,—hold up to me the same facts in the true order of thought.

—Emerson.

MAGAZINES

South, Educational Movement in the, Caroline Matthews. EDUCATIONAL REVIEW, Dec.
Negro Problem, Recent Southern Agitation of the. J. W. Garner. SOUTH ATLANTIC QUARTERLY, Jan.
Color Line in the North, The. I. Ray S. Baker. AMERICAN, Feb.

TO BLACK VOTERS

As between Taft and Johnson vote for Johnson.

As between Taft and LaFollette vote for LaFollette. As between Hughes and Johnson vote for Hughes.

As between FORAKER and Anybody VOTE FOR FORAKER.

As between Taft and Bryan—stay home, 'tis the Devil and the Deep Sea.

Anything to beat Taft except a vote for someone worse than Taft (which is hard to imagine).

In all cases remember that the only party today which treats Negroes as men, North and South, are the Socialists.

Uproot Rooseveltism if it snaps heart strings.

LITTLE BROTHER OF MINE

There lives in Chicago a young man whom I know. This knowing is hardly personal for I have clasped his hand but once, I believe. Our knowing is but a knowing of soul for he is a Brother of Mine: he is a brother of mine in song—his soul within him sings, not freely yet nor powerfully but with promise; he aspires, he knows pain, he has passed through the Valley of the Shadow.

Now, once God in his goodness gave this brother of mine his Chance—made him editor of the *Conservator* on the day he clouded poor Wilkins' mind. I rejoiced. Why? Did I want personal praise in his columns? No, thank God I am not yet quite so small as that. Was it because I wanted him to tear and scold and curse at some real or fancied Enemy? O, little Brother of Mine have I so narrowly revealed my life and purpose that such foul end seems its true interpreting? God forbid! No, I

From *The Horizon: A Journal of the Color Line* 3 (February 1908): 17–20, 21–24.

welcomed James Edgar French to his editing because I said: Now we shall have stalwart, clear, honest writing; a poem here and there, a fine bit quoted, and ever the lofty atmosphere of high and striving ideals.

And what did I see? Halting ambiguous phrases; hesitating assertions, as of one feeling his way cautiously and afraid to talk; neglected columns, careless space-filling rambles; till I came to lift my once stalwart *Conservator* and lay it aside with a sigh. Why? Because it said things that I disagreed with? Because it bestowed praise where I thought no praise due? No, Little Brother of Mine, no; but because it lacked Conviction, Faith, Determination. Just so with the *Age*. Did I agree with Fortune's *Age?* Hardly. But Fortune was, at bottom, honest. At bottom there was Conviction, Faith and Determination, even though half-buried in Subsidy. When then Fortune went and a bag of mush was dumped into his chair, I recorded the loss to the Race.

And now: Did I blame *you*, Brother of Mine for this emasculated *Conservator?* No indeed. I know who owns the *Conservator* stock. I know what narrow bounds and commands were probably laid upon you. I might blame you for accepting the limitations—for not standing up straight and saying: "By God, Sir, I'll be Editor or Nothing." But perhaps this was impracticable. I placed no blame therefore—I simply said: *Lost.* Was I far wrong, Little Brother of Mine?

"KNOW THY PEOPLE"

It is good news that the Colonial Office—whose West African Department is in the hands of an experienced official, possessed, seemingly, of a good deal more imagination and sympathy than permanent officials can usually boast of—has issued instructions to the officials in the various West African dependencies to "collect material for a report on native customs and folk-lore which the Colonial Office hope to draw up under the supervision of some competent anthropologist." This is a suggestion we have ventured to make a great many times, and it is satisfactory to find that the Colonial Office is now of the same opinion. The fountain of all intelligent government by aliens must be a knowledge of the habits, customs, laws, traditions and modes of thought of the people governed. It has often been made a reproach to our handling of subject races that while we excel in the purity of our justice, and in our genuine desire to promote the well-being of the people according to our ideas of what constitutes their well-being, we lack the gift of sympathy, we are too cast-iron in our prejudices, too scornful of what appear to us as mere antediluvianism and superstition, too apt to destroy by the very unimaginative regularity of our rule much of what is romantic and worth preserving in the political and social economy of our subjects. We are inclined to think there is a good deal of truth in these criticisms; and also that, whereas what is good in our rule emanates from the qualities of the race, that which is lacking can be remedied by increased knowledge and systematic investigation. There is always room for improvement, and the action of the Colonial Office seems precisely calculated to effect such improvement on the lines indicated—*African Mail.*

A BOOK

This volume represents a very notable and, we think, an almost unique achievement. A man of pure African blood, a native, and one to whom English is an acquired language, has set himself to provide Englishmen with a statement of West

African customary laws, and has succeeded in doing it, with a firm grasp of English legal principles, a lucid and forcible style (despite some trifling errors in syntax), and in a spirit of pure and exalted African patriotism. The gain to comparative jurisprudence, as in the author's earlier "Fanti Customary Laws," is considerable; the service rendered to students of African political problems is no less.†

When, for example, we learn that according to Fanti Customary Law, there is no such a thing as unowned land, and that all unoccupied land is held by the Native Courts (some people will be surprised to hear that West African natives have a whole hierarchy of regularly constituted Courts) to be attached to the paramount stool, i.e., is a kind of *ager publicus*, those of us who are advocates of native rights, find ourselves in possession of a fact which, if brought to bear upon the interpretation of Articles 34 and 35 of the Berlin Act for the colonization of Africa, would make very short work of the arbitrary claims by which, in the Congo Free State and elsewhere, large tracts of land have been filched from the native tribes on the ground that they were "no-man's-land."

Mr. Sarbah's account of the village community, based on a form of patriarchal power in which the *penin*, or head of the family, is very much more a trustee for his children and kindred than Sir Henry Maine's hard-worked patriarch of early Roman law, is singularly suggestive, and, what is more, thoroughly intelligible, for we are here not in the speculative twilight of Maine's theories, but keeping company with law reports which illustrate and define these things by disputes as to freedom of alienation, etc. The whole of this section stirs deep questions of comparative jurisprudence.

Since Sir Henry Maine brought in the East to redress the balance of the West, and the greatest of legal Philosophers, Ihering, taught us to look to the origins of Roman law, the gaze of scholars has been almost exclusively fixed on the cradle of the Asian plateaux. But, judging by Mr. Sarbah's work, there may be much treasure-trove in the dark hinterlands, and if African dialects found the place in European schools which is occupied by Oriental languages, there is no knowing what the result might bring forth.

Mr. Sarbah makes no attempt to point analogies, and it would be too much to expect him to be acquainted with the work of legal historians like Fustel des Cou-langes, Ihering, Brunner, Lieberman and Maitland; but his clear exposition of Fanti customs continually provokes comparisons of a remarkably close kind on such points as the formalism of native legal procedure, its principles of kinship liability, collective oaths, and even legal trial by battle (now obsolete). It is, however, in the account of the village and tribal constitutions, based on the patriarchal power, that we come in touch with the political purpose of the book.

The author makes it clear that the Fantis possess a highly developed, if comparatively simple, commonwealth, based on the principle of elective kingship—election being usually confined to the blood-royal—and of a council which is essentially representative of the people at large. As Mr. Sarbah plausibly remarks, if these two facts were borne in mind, national sentiment would not so frequently have been outraged by the deportation of West African chiefs on the mistaken assumption that they were despots, nor would the English Government be slow to avail themselves of these tribal councils as organs of opinion. Authority between headman (*odzikoro*), chief (*ohene*) and king (*omanhene*), each with his official stool, is carefully graduated, while in the legal use of the stool and its distinctions between public stool property and family stool property, it is not difficult to discern the elements of a law of capacities and some legal conception not unlike English treatment of the Crown.

Mr. Sarbah's ultimate object is to prove the possibility of grafting the least objectionable features of Crown colony administration—with which he is as little in agreement as the late Miss Kingsley was—on to the native African policy, and at the same time to protest against the encroachments on the latter made by local officials, in defiance, he argues, of the intentions of Parliament and the jurisprudence of the Privy Council. We have no space to follow his reasonings here—they largely turn on the questions of State succession—but we may say that we think his contention that the native jurisdiction is original and not derivative, and therefore cannot be encroached on except by express agreement, is proved.

—*Manchester Guardian*

EDITOR'S NOTE
†The reference is to John Mansah Sarbah's *Fanti Customary Laws* (1897) and his *Fanti National Constitution* (1898). Revised editions of both were published in 1968 by F. Cass Company, London.

15

The Over-Look

Woe to the land shadowing with wings, which is beyond the rivers of Ethiopia:
That sendeth ambassadors by the sea, even in vessels of bulrushes upon the
    waters, saying,
Go ye swift messengers, to a nation scattered and peeled, to a people terrible
    from their beginning hitherto; a nation meted out and trodden down, whose
    land the rivers have spoiled!

Isaiah 18: 1–2.

READING

The magazines are getting silent and suspicious; Baker writes of the "Negroes'
Industrial Position in the North," in the March *American*. The papers meantime are
much alarmed over the Negroes' political attitude. Remember Brownsville! A southerner in a Northern College, Jerome Dowd, has begun an ambitious Sociological
program, with the study of the "Negro Races" (Macmillan), in a fat book, which I
have not yet read.

IDA DEAN BAILEY

She was, in her prime, a woman of regal beauty, and always of commanding
personality—born leader and mother of men. Her strength, her comeliness, her
mighty purity of soul, her perfect candor, and resolute unselfishness, the very
storming of her impetuous power, were all builded on a magnificent scale. She was
born to play a part on a world stage—no narrow pent-up niche of life for her, but
great sweeping vistas and a glorious vision of eternal success.

Only last January, looking Death in the very eye, she wrote me when I asked
her to become joint Secretary with Mrs. Morgan, over the women of the Niagara
Movement: "I have since last night decided to undertake the work. I have many
plans and if I can get strong, they may work out for good. *I never met defeat when
I really tried!*" How splendid a spiritual record was such a memory!

Four things this woman seems to me to have been:

A Woman—with all the tender softness, grace and quick elusive subtlety that
mark her sex. There are men's women, and women's women, but she was both, to
a most surprising degree: the companion and co-worker of men, she had no kind
of masculinity; the leader and *confidante* of women, she was never merely feminine.

From *The Horizon: A Journal of the Color Line* 3 (March 1908): 1, 2–8.

A Mother. What life denied her of physical motherhood, she repaid by an all-embracing desire to mother the world. This half-conscious impulse to succour and guide, protect and defend, often made her seem intrusive and domineering, but once the pure unselfishness of the motive behind it became visible—the sweet motherliness of her striving—and all was forgiven; only the unselfishness of the service lingered in memory.

A Friend. We think of women as things to be loved and wived. We think of friendship as primarily masculine. But Ida Bailey was to an uncounted host, a woman and a friend— a combination, rare but wonderful in its full realization. She was not merely the friend of Success, Wealth and Notoriety,—she was the friend of the Soul itself, even in its sin, failure and disgrace. She picked down after the real man and grappled it and encouraged and cherished it; and she never lost faith in a woman. She showed her loyalty and friendship, not merely by the flattery of praise, but by the candor of criticism, and it was for that we all valued her.

Most people have neither friends nor enemies—they have simply acquaintances. Strong souls have Friends and Enemies. Ida Bailey was strong. Her enemies, who often shrank before the white blaze of her terrible frankness, will breathe more freely now, but her friends will step softly and reverently.

A Leader. She was a leader of the Negro race: one who voluntarily identified herself with its spiritual strivings, felt in her own deep and sensitive soul its shortcomings and oppressions, and pointed the way, pushing, arguing, compelling her friends and acquaintances to follow. She commanded obedience, but she gave herself in turn: money, time, thought and life, so unselfishly, that in the end all welcomed her masterful way. Her home was in a peculiar degree, one of the spiritual centers of Negro civilization in this world.

She is gone. Voiceless, cold, still, and all unmoved is that once quivering, busy, throbbing mass of nerve, and blood and deed. But if somehow and somewhere the Love and Devotion, the wistful Aspiration, tireless Energy and dauntless Courage of that Soul still sweeps all silently the universe of God—forget not, O My Friend, this bit of dust, whereon we struggle still; and through the unveiled Mist of Years, cry forth the mighty justice of our cause before the face of God.

DARWINISM

There was a time in the 19th century when Science was apparently dead set against unfortunate or "inferior" races. All the world of Darwinism was glib about "undeveloped" races and the "Survival of the Fittest." Later and more careful interpretation of the real facts is putting a different face on the truth: we have long since learned, for instance, that the "fit" in survival is not necessarily the Best or the most Decent—it may be simply the most Impudent, or the biggest Thief or Liar. We are getting even further than that: Alfred Wallace, who shares with Darwin the honor of conceiving the newer evolutionary doctrine, now declares that physically and in essential mental structure, the Advanced Races are not superior to the earliest barbarians; and that among the present races of man, none can be scientifically demonstrated to be physically inferior to others. In other words he agrees with Boas, that genius and civilization are not the property of the white man.

STRAKER

The passing of Augustus Straker calls for some tribute of respect. He represented the rapidly dwindling number of Reconstructive actors, and one, too, who never gave up his ideals and never crawled and kow-towed to the "New South." He was born in Barbadoes, in 1842, and came to the United States in 1868, in response to a call for teachers and ministers. He studied for orders in the Episcopal Church, but meeting its miserable discriminations turned to the law. This launched him into politics and eventually he became inspector of Customs in Charleston, South Carolina and afterward a member of the Legislature. After the Hampton revolution of 1876 he became law partner of the brilliant Robert Brown Elliot, and finally disgusted with the South he removed to Detroit, Michigan, where he was elected to the position of Judge of the Commissioner's Court of the City and was re-elected for several terms.

BRYAN

It looks like Bryan and Taft. In that case the Black voter must do some thinking. Personally Bryan's record on the Negro is clear. He has made few if any specific references to the problem. Yet even in this he is infinitely better than Taft, whose North Carolina speech said: the Negro is out of politics; the Republicans are willing to keep him out, therefore "Forget him." As between the two men, Bryan is certainly preferable to the Coward of Brownsville. As to parties, men ask: "what has the Democratic party done for the Negro?" About as much as the Negro has done for the Democratic party, and about as much as the Republicans are doing for us. If the Republican party insults the black man by nominating Taft, *vote for Bryan.*

MULATTOES

The inevitable fusion of races brought into contact, despite the wishes of one or both, is being illustrated again in South Africa, and there as here it is bound up with fundamental questions of human rights. A correspondent in the London *Times* writes:

> Whereas in the Transvaal, in the Orange Free State, and in Natal there was always a tendency to refuse to grant even to the educated native the privileges of citizenship, in Cape Colony it has always been assumed that colour must be no bar to the possession of those privileges.
> "Equal rights for every civilized man south of the Zambesi": that was how Rhodes summarized the principle. But the principle itself had been adopted by Cape Colony long before Rhodes expressed it in a sentence of characteristic bluntness. And the question that inevitably suggests itself is:—"Why did Cape Colony adopt a principle, in dealing with the native question, which is almost diametrically opposed to the principle adopted by the other South African colonies?" To that there is only one possible answer. And it is this. That Cape Colony—as far as the native question goes—is years ahead of the other South African States in her development. She has a large "coloured" population. Very many of the old Dutch families; many, too, of the old English families, have in their veins a strong strain of coloured blood. The process has gone so far that there is now a large "coloured" population—ranging through all the shades, from almost pure white to quite aboriginal black—throughout Cape Colony, with the result that—in Cape Colony at least—it is quite impossible to draw a color line which would be legally enforceable; though socially, as far at least as the upper classes are concerned, the line is in practice very rigidly drawn.

So that Cape Colony has already had to face what South Africa as a whole will have to face in the future—the fusion of the white and black races. This fusion may be a very deplorable fact. Its results as they are visible in Cape Colony today, are certainly not edifying. But it is inevitable.

The inevitable outcome is as clear here as it is in the United States: Negroes are going to be men, with every right accorded to modern men. It is written in the stars. It is coming. It must come. We may not live to see it, but Rome was not built in a day.

16

The Over-Look

And ye shall succor men;
'Tis nobleness to serve;
Help them who cannot help again;
Beware from right to swerve.
—R. W. Emerson

ARTICLES AND BOOKS

The Social Disability of the Jew. Edwin J. Kuh. ATLANTIC MONTHLY.

The South after the War. Carl Schurz. MCCLURE'S.

My African Journey. Right Hon. Winston Spencer Churchill. STRAND MAGAZINE.

The Brownsville Investigation. Senator J. B. Foraker. NORTH AMERICAN REVIEW.

Africa, Across Central, by Boat. E. A. Forbes. WORLD'S WORK.

India, The Unrest in. Percevel Landon. WORLD'S WORK.

Lincoln, Recollections of. O. O. Howard. CENTURY.

Mulatto, The tragedy of the. Ray S. Baker. AMERICAN.

(April issues of Magazines except otherwise noted.)

Sectionalism Unmasked. Compiled by Henry Edwin Tremain. Bonnell, Silver & Co. 12mo, pp 322. $1.25 net.

Justice to the Jew. The Story of What He has done for the World. By Madison C. Peters. Revised edition; 12 mo, pp 244. McClure Co. 75 cts net.

A Guide to the West Indies and the Bermudas. By Frederick A. Ober. Illus. and with maps, 16 mo. pp 525. Dodd, Mead & Co, $2.25 net.

Who's Who in America. 1908-1909. Edited by Albert Nelson Marquis. Chicago: A. N. Marquis & Co. $4 net.

White man's work in Asia and Africa: A discussion of the main difficulties of the color Question. By Leonard Alston. Longmans. 1907. 136 pp. (Maitland Prize essay, Cambridge University, '06.)

The United States in the 20th Century. Leroy-Beaulieu, Pierre. Funk & Wagnalls 1907. (Contains chapter on The Negro Population and the Race Question. pp 36-47)

———

From *The Horizon: A Journal of the Color Line* 3 (April 1908): 1–8.

In Who's Who, I have found the names of nearly thirty Negro Americans whom I know, and there are probably others. Leroy-Beaulieu knows very little about us. Baker's article is the best yet; and Foraker says for the soldiers:

> To find men guilty upon the evidence secured is to disregard, to violate, and to reverse every recognized rule for weighing evidence. It is not only to hold these men as murderers and perjurers, but to assert that Major Penrose and all his officers, than whom there are none in the army more honorable, upright and reliable, were not worthy of credence when they testified under oath that they believed their men had told the truth and were entirely innocent.

TAFT

We who are of the true faith, as we firmly believe, and would rather vote for Bryan than Taft must remember that our chief work in the next campaign is to convince men as honest as we who cannot see that our proposed action is wise. We must not make the tactical error of losing our temper or calling these men names. We believe them wrong, but we also believe that they, as well as we, desire the interests of our race and of our country. With such men we must argue earnestly in the next few months.

We exclude from consideration, of course, office-holders, and office-seekers. We do not condemn these classes—their calling is honorable and their ambition may be laudable; but in the nature of the case an office-holder cannot speak, or always think, freely. When therefore one abuses us, we sit silent. It is not he that speaks, it is his salary.

To the mass of thinking Negro voters, however, who are not making a living out of politics, and who regard political activity not as a vocation but as a way to Freedom and Justice—to these we may lay down certain considerations:

1. The Negro is and ought to be a Republican, since he owes his freedom, enfranchisement and civil rights to that party.

2. If then the Republican party nominates any one, who in a reasonable degree stands for the traditions of this party, the Negro should vote for him.

He may not be the Negro's tried and true friend like Foraker, or a just man to all races like Hughes; but if he is a Republican and reasonably faithful to the past, vote for him.

3. But! We know that we are today losing the things which the older Republican party gave us: we are losing our Vote, our Freedom, our Civil Rights. Who are taking them away? Southern Democrats and Northern sympathizers. These sympathizers are right in the Republican party, and their views are voiced by Theodore Roosevelt and William Taft.

4. If this reactionary wing of the Republicans triumphs, we are in grave danger. We are sentenced for a century to Jim Crow cars, peonage and disfranchisement. This is proven. With Republicans in control of all branches of the government all these things have increased and flourished and Taft has told the South: "Rest easy—it is all right."

5. These reactionaries can only triumph by Negro votes; we had in 1900 the balance of power in the following Northern states:

States	Negro Vote
Connecticut	4,576
Illinois	29,762
Iowa	4,441
Kansas	14,695
Massachusetts	10,456
Michigan	5,193
Nebraska	2,298
New Jersey	21,474
New York	31,425
Ohio	31,235
Pennsylvania	51,668
Rhode Island	2,765
Total, 1900	209,987
Probable total, 1908	250,000

6. Depending thus on our votes, why do the Republicans contemptuously ignore us? Would they ignore two or three hundred thousand Germans or Irishmen or Italians? No. Why not? They do not *own* them—they think they own us. They do not own me. Do they own you?

7. Is a vote for Democracy impossible for a Negro? No. Northern Democrats are as friendly as Northern Republicans. Southern Democrats are our sworn enemies, but they are not fools. If Bryan wins by Negro votes, and if Democracy can stay in power only by Negro votes, will the Democratic party flout us? If you think so read the Columbia (S. C.) *State* of April 1, 1908. Indeed unless we do get some hold on the Democrats what mercy can we expect at their hands? It is foolhardy to let any party remain unobligated to us.

8. Friends we are not deserting the Republican party—the Republican party is deserting us. If we want its power, we must make ourselves necessary to it. If we are willing to sell our liberty for six minor political offices thrown us as a sop at the command of a traitorous and cringing Boss, then our liberty is gone. But if we stand, ballot in hand, ready to punish the party that insults and neglects us, it will learn in time to treat us as men and not as dogs.

CHARLES CUTHBERT HALL†

It seems almost cruel to take from us so staunch and true a man as Charles Cuthbert Hall and leave the cowards. How few public men today dare to take the righteous stand on this mighty race problem. With one accord they dodge and quibble and hedge: One has bought land or securities, and one must prove the ox-minds around him, and one has married a Southern wife. Truly we shall find our friends of tomorrow in the highways and hedges. But now and then a great strong man stands straight in his boots, whether in New York or New Orleans, and talks the gospel of Jesus Christ.

Such a one was Charles Cuthbert Hall. He believed in liberty for all men, black, brown and white, and he not only believed, but spoke and acted his belief. He spread the gospel in India, not as a narrow creed-choked bigot, but as an educated gentleman talking to gentlemen and not to dogs. He believed in educating Negroes not merely as servants but as men. He believed in the social equality of equal souls.

I have seen him standing and receiving in gracious courtesy black and white and brown men and women and greeting them as friends.

God rest his soul!

THE SOUTHERN ELECTORATE

The Southern ballot is purified. White "civilization" is triumphant. If you do not believe it look at the swearing Jeff Davis and the murderous Heflin; behold the sparring of John Sharp Williams, the brawling of Tillman, and the yells of Vardaman; watch the valiant "war claim" grafters, and doughty epithet-throwers in Congress. Witness the chaste English these representatives of the New South use. Recall their wide learning and lofty patriotism, and then compare them with the displaced Negro congressmen—Bruce, Rapier, Lynch and the gifted Elliot. Shades of Calhoun and Toombs—the South is redeemed.

Eight new Governmental schools were opened in the colony of Southern Nigeria during the year 1906. At present there are thirty-one Government schools, four of them girls' schools in the colony and protectorate, five in the Western Province, seventeen in the Central Province, and nine in the Eastern Province. All these schools appear to be going well, and it is additional evidence, if, indeed, any be needed, of the keen desire of the native population to acquire all the learning they can to enable them to keep up with the progress of civilization.— *African Mail.*

According to the Liberian mail just to hand the inauguration of President Barclay was an affair of much brilliance. The period was memorable also owing to the fact that this was the Jubilee year of the Republic. The President paid a warm tribute to the Legislative and to the Judiciary branches in the course of his remarks. He also touched upon the importance of the relations of his Republic with America. In this connection he remarked that "while American philanthropists had helped greatly in the development of the country, and while American sentiment is clearly interested in our prosperity, yet American diplomacy has never given the Liberian Government the effective support which at times it has needed."—*African Mail.*

EDITOR'S NOTE
†Charles Cuthbert Hall (1852–1908) served for 25 years as Pastor of the First Presbyterian Church in Brooklyn, N.Y. From 1897 until his death, he was president of the Union Theological Seminary; he also served in India from 1902 to 1906. Among his best known books was *Christ and the Human Race* (1906).

17

The Over-Look

PERIODICALS FOR MAY

Negro Parties in the North. Ray S. Baker. AMERICAN.
Prohibition in the South. Frank Foxcroft. ATLANTIC.
Races, The Strength of. C. Woods Hutchinson. WORLD'S WORK.
Negro Homes. Booker T. Washington. CENTURY.
Reconstruction, First Days of. Carl Schurz. MCCLURE.
Indian as a Laborer, The. C. H. Forbes–Lindsay. CRAFTSMAN.

WELL-WISHER

This letter has come to me:

Chicago, May 2nd, 1908.

My dear Dr. Du Bois,

It would be a good thing for you to talk more about the bumptious negroes up in the North. You give a great deal of advice but never say a word to this offensive brand of your race. They make more enemies and feeling against the colored man in the North than any other cause. One of them offsets the good influence of a dozen polite colored men. They always want to "show off," are loud-mouthed, flashily dressed, and want to be where they are not wanted, or do what they can't. Often they are very impertinent, chesty and "fresh." I know the *great harm* they are doing your race in the North, and I trust you will advise them to make themselves less obnoxious. Yours truly,

A Well Wisher.

Bumptious people are trying. The loud-mouthed and flashily dressed do much to spoil an otherwise bearable world. America has invented the striking words "chesty" and "fresh" because they express something peculiarly American but not on that account the less obnoxious or harmful. Therefore I pass this anonymous note on. Heed it, my brothers, it has its grain of truth and sense.

And now you Mr. Well-Wisher: What is this you describe so well and complain of so bitterly? It is aught but that consciousness of power, that ill-balanced but just ambition, that sense of boundless but unrealized possibilities which characterizes all Youth—the youth of the individual as well as the youth of a race or of a nation? Do you know that the same thing which you complain of in Northern Negroes, Europe complains of in North Americans, and men complain of in boys? Only last summer I saw a mob of American tourists—loud-mouthed, flashily dressed, impertinent, "chesty" and "fresh"—swoop down onto a little Scotch steamer on Loch Katrine near lovely Ellen's Isle. Oh! it was worse than painful, and the Scotch and

From *The Horizon: A Journal of the Color Line* 3 (May 1908): 1–3.

56

English and I, fled to the gun-wales and sat silent. And yet we understood them: they were not wicked but untrained; they did not mean to hurt the finer sensibilities of their fellow-men, they simply were crudely expressing themselves in a painfully inarticulate way. They were a tired, stunted, gasping set of school teachers, farmers and merchants and they wanted Air. How ought they to be received? With kicks and cuffs and ostracism, or with silent tolerance and hope?

What is more trying than that boy of eighteen or twenty who knows it all? Who sets the fashions, kicks the cat, and contradicts the Lord! And yet—and yet—don't kill him, don't suppress him; don't even insist on "advising" him to make himself less "obnoxious." Wait! Look! Listen! Let him grow; he may be Martin Luther bursting his chrysalis, or Alexander Dumas trying his wings; he may foreshadow a mighty people in travail.

18

The Over-Look

They are slaves who fear to speak
For the fallen and the weak;
They are slaves who will not choose
Hatred, scoffing and abuse,
Rather than in silence shrink
From the truth they needs must think.
They are slaves who dare not be
In the right with two or three.

Lowell.

BOOKS AND PERIODICALS

What the White Race May Learn from the Indian. By George Wharton James. Illus.,
   large 8 vo, pp 269. Chicago, Forbes & Co. $1.50 net.
Southern Agriculture. By F. S. Earle. Illus., 12mo, pp 297. Macmillan Co. $1.25.

———

Brazil, Land of Coffee. Arthur Ruhl. SCRIBNER.
Dumas, Alexandre. Gamaliel Bradford, Jr. ATLANTIC.
President Johnson and his War on Congress. Carl Schurz. McCLURE.
The Negro in Politics. Ray S. Baker. AMERICAN.
Negro as Business Man, The. T. J. Calloway. WORLD'S WORK.
The Growing South. E. A. Alderman. WORLD'S WORK

From time to time I have praised Baker's articles in the *American* although
usually here and there I found a bit to criticize and now and then I heard a false
note: but for the article in the June *American* I have nothing but unstinted praise.
It is a strong honest statement made by a man whose heart is right and whose head
is level. Buy it. Read it. Tell your enemies.

Ruhl's astonishment as to lack of color line in Brazil is entertaining.

TAFT

Gentlemen, it has struck twelve. It is High Noon for the Negro voter of the
United States of America. By the time my readers see this, William H. Taft will in
all probability be the Republican nominee for President. What are the principles
for which he stands?

From *The Horizon: A Journal of the Color Line* 3 (June 1908): 1–7, 8.

He approves of disfranchisement laws of the South "conceding that the laws now in force in this state (North Carolina) and other parts of the South were intended either by their terms or by their mode of execution to exclude the ignorant colored voter from the franchise with rigor, and to allow the ignorant white voter, though actually unfitted for the franchise to exercise it." (Greensboro, N. C., speech, July 10, 1906.)

He does not want Negro Universities founded "to furnish the higher mental education to a people not fitted to enjoy it or make it useful." (Tuskegee, April 4, 1906.)

He praises Abraham Lincoln for opposing Negro suffrage. (Grand Rapids, Feb. 13, 1908.)

He declares that the fifteenth amendment has been unsuccessful; that the disfranchisement of the Negro is better than "violent methods" and that the "greatest friend" the Negro "is likely to have" is the Southern white man who "knows his *value to the South!*" (Kansas City, Mo., Feb. 10, 1908.)

These are not the final words of Mr. Taft, nor all of his qualifications of those words. But they do convey the spirit of his remarks, namely, that Industrial Education, disfranchisement and surrender to the demands of the white South is the proper program for the Negro today. In addition to this, Remember Brownsville.

Of course there is the other side: Recently at Fisk University Mr. Taft, candidate for President, slightly revised his attitude toward Negro higher education, and letter after letter has come to me darkly hinting at tremendous proofs of the righteousness of Mr. Taft's Brownsville attitude at the proper time. But when all is said and done, the flat fact remains that William Taft represents that class of Americans who believe that:

Negroes are less than Men;
Few of them ought to vote;
Their education should be restricted;
Their opportunities should be limited;
Their fate must be left to the South;
Their "value" is their money value to their neighbors;
On occasion they may be treated like dogs, (*vide* Brownsville).

This is the platform in plump, plain English. What is the difference between this and the Democratic Platform? There is no difference.

It is High Noon, brethren—the Clock has struck Twelve. What are we going to do? I have made up my mind. You can do as you please: you are free, sane, and twenty-one. If between two parties who stand on identically the same platform you can prefer the party who perpetrated Brownsville, well and good! But I shall vote for Bryan.

"They are slaves who will not choose
Hatred, scoffing and abuse,
Rather than in silence shrink
From the truth they needs must think."

UNION

There are now four organizations standing for essentially the same things:

The Niagara Movement,
The Afro-American Council,

The Negro American Political League,
The Negro Academy.

Each organization once had its *raison d'etre*: the Niagara Movement crystallized
a faint dissatisfaction into an organized and articulate protest. The Council is the
first and oldest of these organizations. The Political League is a union of certain
men in these two organizations to effect one great object. The Academy is a step
toward Science and Art.

The difficulty with all these organizations is money. The combined annual dues
of all of them amount to fourteen dollars a year—a prohibitive fee for the mass of
colored men. This fee however could easily be well spent, but, as it is, it is wasted
by duplication of work, and members are wasted by duplication of energy. Three
of the organizations are doing very largely the same things, and all want the same
things. This was not true five years ago—scarcely so a year ago. Today it is true,
and today is the time for a union of forces.

The Niagara Movement meets at Oberlin late in August, 1908. As executive
head of that Movement I hereby invite the Afro-American Council, the Negro
Political League, and the Negro Academy to meet at the same time and place. The
Time is opportune, at the beginning of a fateful presidential campaign. The *Place*
is auspicious—the Capital of the Underground Railroad, and the place of the first
efforts for the higher education of the Negro. Will Waldron, Walters, and Grimke
join me here with the avowed object of consolidating there and then these four
great organizations? That the sincerity and unselfishness of this invitation may be
unquestioned, I hereby pledge myself to accept no office in the gift of the united
organizations.

TWELFTH NIGHT

The seniors of Atlanta University played "Twelfth Night" for their class day,
and played it wonderfully. Six hundred people sat and saw them: the fair Olivia
did her part with womanly grace and womanish daintiness. Sir Tobey brought forth
peals of laughter, and the gay Maria captivated her listeners. Yet all these were
Negroes, trained (and rarely trained) by one of our own blood and lineage; bringing
out as so seldom is brought out, but so often will be, the tremendous artistic and
dramatic power of a suppressed and soul-starved race who despite all bonds must
one day be free. Well done, Our Lady of Atlanta.

O SOUTHLAND!
BY JAMES W. JOHNSON

Oh Southland! O Southland!
    Have you not heard the call,
The trumpet blown, the world made known
    To the Nations, one and all?
The watchword, the hope-word,
    Salvation's present plan?
A gospel new, for all—for you:
    Man shall be saved by man.
        New York Independent.

19

The Over-Look

Behold!
The Sphinx is Africa. The bond
Of silence is upon her. Old
And white with tombs, and rent and shorn;
With raiment wet with tears and torn,
And trampled on, yet all untamed.

Miller.

FREE

At last I am free. Around me stretch the woods and water. I live and walk and sleep unhampered in the fresh sweet air. No longer am I thrall to starch and rigorous raiment. I snatch my food sparkling from the brook, red from the bush, or dig it cold from the ground. I know neither visitors nor newspapers. The twittering wren awakens me and the lonely whip-poor-will sings me drowsily to rest. Problem? There are no problems, and I am free.

THE HORIZON

The problem of the Negro periodical is nearing solution. Certain points which were problematical yesterday are clearly established today. For instance, in numbers of cases it has been clearly proven that given a good local constituency and a man with the newspaper gift, a small sheet can be made to pay moderately. Based on this local success the paper may reach out and cover a region and even large portions of the nation, but such papers are hampered by the demands of the local constituency, so that three-fourths of the reading matter is worthless outside their own city.

To step beyond the locality and establish a national journal on a paying basis is difficult and has not yet been done successfully. The most brilliant attempt was the *Voice of the Negro*, which so richly deserved success and might have won it but for underhanded treachery. The *Moon* was another short lived attempt.

Newspapers and magazines for the general public have achieved national circulation by two methods: a high subscription price or multitudinous advertisements. Both of these methods are at present impossible for the Negro; we are a poor people. The only other methods are these: to seek secret subsidy or openly to make up the annual deficit.

From *The Horizon: A Journal of the Color Line* 4 (July 1908): 1–8.

Subsidy is degrading and dangerous because it implies the secret buying of a paper's policy by persons unknown and often unsuspected by the readers. When Negroes know that today editorials are being written at the dictation of that same despicable Hitchcock who made "lily-whiteism" triumph at Chicago, they lose faith in their "Negro" paper.

The other method is openly making up the business deficit. When the HORIZON was established the proprietors knew it would not pay. It appealed to a few, it was "different." They carefully estimated the annual deficit, made it up among themselves and gave their services free. The result has been gratifying. The paper has had a small but growing circulation, has paid for four-fifths of its expense and elicited respect if not approval.

The time has now come when the proprietors face this problem: the magazine should be enlarged and broadened so as in some measure to supply the crying need of a national monthly. Yet such a monthly cannot today be made wholly self-supporting. Of course it might struggle on by appeals, campaign funds and graft—but as a straight-out, independent, business proposition a national Negro magazine will not pay yet. In ten, perhaps five years, it will. Today it will not. Yet we need a journal, not as a matter of business but as a matter of spiritual life and death. This means that somebody must foot the bill. The deficit must be made as small as the best business management will allow, but that deficit must be paid openly and regularly by those who believe in the principles of the HORIZON.

Therefore the proprietors of the HORIZON propose that for one year beginning September 1st, 1908, 100 guarantors pledge themselves to pay $25 each in such installments and at such times as they may designate to guarantee the support of this magazine. These guarantors are to become the proprietors of the HORIZON and the enlarged magazine will be conducted by an executive committee appointed by them.

The names of the first four guarantors follow. We hope to add to the number each month:

1. F. H. M. Murray
2. L. M. Hershaw
3. W. E. B. DuBois
4. F. L. McGhee

THE NEGRO VOTER

During the next three months I propose to have a series of five heart to heart talks with the Negro-American voter. I am assuming that he is free, twenty-one and unpurchaseable. I assume that he is intelligent and proposes to vote according to his reason and not according to the dictation of a Boss. Those who are enslaved, bought, idiotic or afraid will not be interested in these remarks.

Talk Number One

THESIS: That aside from special considerations of race, the policy of the Democratic party is the best policy for the Nation.

The Democratic party today stands for the strict regulation of corporate wealth, for the freedom and independence of brown and black men in the West Indies and the Philippines, for the right of labor to strive for higher wages and better working conditions, for a low tariff, and for the abolition of all special privilege.

No group of Americans is feeling the crushing grasp of corporate wealth more than Negroes. Not a single law made in the South hinders a railroad from giving black men just as good accommodations as whites, and yet not a single railroad does this. The Pullman monopoly recently in the Niagara Movement case paid over $100 rather than give a colored lady a $2 seat. And yet its president is Abraham Lincoln's son!

Through-out the South great corporations are more and more grasping and grinding, and crushing Negro labor in mines, mills, lumber camps, and brick-yards and then posing for praise in giving them work at rates twenty-five per cent below decent living. If this nation does not assume control of corporations, corporations will assume control of this nation. Have you no interest in this Mr. Black Worker? Did you notice that while the Republicans weakened and retreated in this fight at Chicago, the Democrats stood to their guns at Denver?

The Rape of Cuba, and the Conquest of the Philippines are the blackest things in recent American history—fit to be written down beside the Seminole "wars," and the looting of Mexico. Who freed Cuba? Black men. Who freed the Philippines? Brown men. Who snatched the victory from both and kicked the "niggers" back to their places? The Republican party. Who is conspiring to perpetuate "white" rule in both lands? The Republican party. Who promises freedom and independence to both? The Democratic party.

The cause of organized labor is the cause of black laborers. Tens of thousands of black men belong to the unions and more are joining each day. That the Republicans are the foes of organized labor is shown by the record of Taft, Cannon, and Sherman.

What interest has any black man in a high tariff? He is a farm laborer and the farm has no protection; he is a house servant and as such benefits in no degree; as a small business and professional man he has no protected products; the protected industries are the manufacturing plants—how many Negroes work there? On the other hand as a consumer the Negro is bearing the burden of all this tariff tare in his food, fuel, and furniture. The Negro's interest in a low tariff is clearer than in the case of any single American group.

And finally every influence and move toward greater democratic freedom, wider popular power and abolition of special privilege is, whether intended or not, an inevitable step toward the emancipation of black men as well as white.

Therefore, *vote for Bryan.*

AN AFRICAN ON HIS RACE

The stirring lectures delivered recently by Dr. Blyden have aroused a considerable amount of interest in England, and have excited the patriotic feelings of his compatriots in West Africa. Barrister Casely Hayford has written a long letter to the *Sierra Leone Weekly News* in which he discusses some of the problems raised by the learned Doctor. His remarks on educational matters are full of sound advice to his brethren, and we cannot do better than reproduce a portion of them here:

"The crux of the educational question, as it affects the African, is that Western methods denationalized him. He becomes a slave to foreign ways of life and thought. He will desire to be a slave no longer. So far is this true that the moment the unspoilt educated African shews initiative and asserts an individuality, his foreign mentor is irritated by the phenomenon. In September 1905, public events on the Gold Coast led me to write in the local Press as follows: 'We feel, secondly, that the educated native is unduly maligned for Party purposes. It is the same cry as the educated Welsh, Irish, or Scotch. In any case, it is a childish cry—a sign of weakness. Does a native cease to be a native when he is educated? But for the educated native, where would the unsophisticated native be? Hence the weakness of the cry—the shibboleth of the 'educated native.' Heaven grant that the educated native may never be wanting in his duty to his less privileged brethren or betray their trust in him.'

"But let there be no mistake about the matter. The foregoing strictly applies to the unspoilt cultured African. The other type is no good to anybody. The superfine African gentleman, who, at the end of every second or third year, talks of a run to Europe lest there should be a nervous breakdown, may be serious or not, but is bound in time to be refined off the face of the African continent.

"And now I come to the question of questions. How may the West African be trained so as to preserve his national identity and race instincts?

"As a precautionary measure, I would take care to place the educational seminary in a region far beyond the reach of the influence of the Coast. If I were founding a national University for the Gold Coast and for Ashanti, I would make a suitable suburb of Kumasi the centre. But why do I speak of a national University? For the simple reason that you cannot educate a people unless you have a suitable training ground. A Tuskegee Institute is very useful in its way, but where would you get the teachers unless you drew them from the ranks of the University-trained men? And since even the teachers must be first locally trained, the highest training ground becomes a necessity."—*African Mail.*

20

The Over-Look

And Gideon said unto him
O my Lord, if the Lord be with us
Why then is all this befallen us?
And where be all His miracles?
—Judges VI: 13.

THE GUARANTORS

The undersigned agree to pay twenty-five dollars each next year toward the publication of the enlarged HORIZON, of which they will become proprietors:

1. F. H. M. MURRAY, Alexandria, Va.
2. L. M. HERSHAW, Washington, D. C.
3. W. E. B. DuBois, Atlanta, Ga.
4. F. L. McGHEE, St. Paul, Minn.
5. JOSEPH SHERWOOD, St. Paul, Minn.
6. L. R. DIGGS, Frankfort, Ky.

We want one hundred guarantors. Please write us as soon as you decide.

NEGRO VOTE

Talk Number Two

THESIS: That the ballot is a power to be used not to secure "jobs" for a few men, but to establish certain great principles of justice and sound policy.

If Mr. Bryan is elected president will he appoint as many Negroes to office as Mr. Roosevelt has? I do not know, nor do I particularly care; for this, though a matter of some importance, is subsidiary to the vastly greater questions of economic and social justice for which we fight. Ten thousand Negroes at most are interested directly in office-holding; ten thousand thousand are interested in being able to walk and ride and work under decent conditions. I want no man appointed to any office simply because he is a Negro. I want him appointed because he is a capable man. President Bryan will find that no Southern white man has been able to conduct an Internal Revenue office better than Rucker of Atlanta; that some of the most efficient clerks in Washington are black; that the Post Offices of the South are largely in colored men's hands, through competitive examination. In other words

From *The Horizon: A Journal of the Color Line* 4 (August 1908): 1–8.

he will find that capability knows no color line. If therefore President Bryan is an honest man, as I believe he is, he will know no color line in his appointments.

But this is a subsidiary. We Negroes are voting, or we should be voting, not to secure jobs for the few but to secure justice for all; we are voting to break down and wipe out and utterly abolish the most asinine and brutal and cruel of human distinctions: the *Color Line*—the monstrous heathenism that judges a human being not by the size of his soul but by the hue of his hide. Would God, we could vote on the thing directly! Would God we could choose between two parties—one of which stood for Caste, and the other for Freedom. But one cannot. We must choose between two parties, both of which represent largely things which we and all decent citizens ought to hate and despise.

What then? We must still vote. We must choose between two evils, but choose the larger good that is intermixed. That is what the power of the ballot means. It takes years for the voter in a republic to get a *chance* to vote for his greatest desire. It took England a generation to get a chance to vote on the corn laws—it took America 40 years to get a chance to vote on slavery; it may take us a hundred years to get a chance to vote squarely on the color-line; but the chance will come and we will hasten the chance by voting intelligently and not blindly and ignorantly at every preliminary step.

Moreover, in voting for justice to Negroes we are not voting injustice to whites. On the contrary, the salvation of white America lies in justice to Black America. Thus we act and vote nationally and not racially, from the most patriotic motives and for the sake of a country which belongs to us far more thoroughly and intimately than it belongs to any other group of Americans.

When therefore the 300,000 free black voters approach the ballot box next November let it be clear in their minds:

> Vote for Principles, not Jobs,
> Vote for Principles, not Parties,
> Vote for Principles, not Men.

No Party can claim gratitude for past services—gratitude belongs to the Principles for which a Party stands. When it deserts those principles it forfeits all claim to gratitude. A party is not a Person to be loved or revered or hated. It is a Machine for registering the Will of the Majority. When it refuses to register that will, it is not only the privilege, it is the bounden duty of the majority to call another machine. To vote "solid" against your convictions is to be an ass.

Standing then in the presence of the Republican and Democratic parties we have to ask ourselves: *not,* which party stands for our principles—neither does; *but,* the triumph of which of these two parties will in the long run bring the triumph of our principles? The answer must be: the triumph of the Democratic party, because:

> 1. The Democratic policy as to the Tariff, Corporations, Imperialism, Labor and Privilege is the better policy.
> 2. Because the Republican party has forefeited its claim to the Negro's vote.
> 3. Because two-thirds of the Democrats (that is, the Northern Democracy) have long deserved our support, and would do more to deserve it if the Solid Negro vote did not put them in slavery to the Solid South.

Talk Number Three

THESIS: That the Republican Party has forfeited its claim to the Negro's vote.

First, a word as to the past:

The Republican party never, as a party, opposed slavery.

The Republican party was responsible for many of the worst "Black Laws" against Free Negroes.

The Republican party was willing to fight and end the War and leave slavery as they found it.

When the Republican party was unable to win the War without Negro soldiers or to elect its candidates without Negro votes, it freed and enfranchised the Negro. For this it deserves credit and the debt has been paid by the unswerving loyalty of Negro voters for forty years, but when the Republican party felt no longer absolutely dependent on Negro voters, it basely deserted the black voters, whom it had shamelessly debauched in Reconstruction times, and winked ponderously at the Crime of '76.

But let all that go. Parties have no Past. They live and work in the Present. What of the present attitude of the Republican party toward Negroes?

A. With full control of all branches of the government, it has not only allowed the disfranchisement of the Negro voters of the South but has sent Mr. Taft to tell the Southerners that their course of action, while not ideal, is justifiable.

B. With full control of all branches of the government, it has not only allowed an arbitrary and unjust separation of interstate travellers but has winked at the subjection of Negro passengers to insult, discomfort, humiliation and physical injury.

C. With full control of the courts it has allowed the punishment of alleged Negro criminals, not only without due process of law, but under circumstances of such atrocity and barbarism as have shocked and continue to shock civilization.

D. With full control of the executive and the courts, and with full knowledge of the fact that Negroes are still bought and sold like cattle in the South, treated in numberless cases like dogs, and even held in actual slavery—knowing this, the Republican party stirred neither hand nor foot until foreign governments intervened, and then the party rescued Negroes only where this was unavoidable in the protection of Italians and Greeks.

E. In its own party government the Republicans have repeatedly excluded black voters because they were black and finally gave formal and official sanction to "Lily-Whitism" at its last convention.

F. In an official Presidential message the Republican party has laid down the rule that Negroes do not need higher training but that education fitting them to be laborers, servants and menials is best suited to the race; and finally:

G. Because a few blacks were suspected of treating Southerners as Southerners treated them, without trial or hearing, Theodore Roosevelt dismissed from the United States Army in disgrace not only those suspected but scores of others never accused, denied them the ordinary rights of American citizens and even tried to contravene the constitution—and all this to tarnish the hitherto unblemished record of a soldiery who saved the Union and saved Roosevelt himself on San Juan Hill; and this too the deed of a man who wishes to defend thieving Harvard oarsmen and swaggering West Pointers because they are white!

What excuse does Mr. Taft offer? He "with-held the execution of the President's order thirty-six hours", and then proceeded to execute that which his very hesitation shows he knew to be an unjust and ungenerous blunder. It is this Magnificent

Cowardice that asks the suffrages of ten million black men. They will answer Noverber 3, 1908.

This is the record of the Republican party; and yet in the face of it, solemnly every four years, the party has assured the Negro of its love and determination to do the very things it has persistently neglected to do. Thus the Negro plank of the Republican platform has become a standing joke, and Negro voters are looked upon as fools, too amiable to bolt, and too venal to be feared by a Hitchcock.

Blessed the dead in spirit, our brave dead;
   Not passed but perfected:
Who tower up to mystical full bloom
From self as from a known alchemic tomb;
Who out of wrong
Run forth with laughter and a broken thong;
   Who win from pain their strange and
    flawless grant
Of peace anticipant.

                           —Guiney.

21

The Over-Look

Alone self-poised, henceforward man
Must labor—must resign
His all too human creeds, and scan
Simply the way divine.

—Arnold.

NIAGARA MOVEMENT

OBERLIN, OHIO, SEPTEMBER 2, 1908.

The Niagara Movement at its fourth annual meeting congratulates ten million Negro Americans on their unparalleled opportunity to lead the greatest moral battle of modern times—the fight for the abolition of the color line. In Europe, Asia and Africa the revolt against mere denomination of color and race have begun. The triumph of the highest civilization is the hope of all races, and that civilization is not and never was the property of any one race or color.

The modern attempt to make it so is the last gasp of barbarism, and has caused a moral deterioration which today threatens the peace and progress of the world. Nowhere has the fearful cost of using crime and lies as a weapon to force races into subjection been so apparent as right here in the United States. This nation has stolen the black man's labor, and so learned theft; it has lied away the liberties of black litigants, and so learned lawlessness; it has prostituted the ballot and so shaken the foundation of Democracy. Fellow Americans, does it pay? Is the superiority of the white race demonstrated by burning human beings, lynching innocent working-men, stealing black men's votes and insulting black women?

The program laid down by the Negro haters of America is the most tremendous mistake this nation ever made. It is uncivilized, illogical and wrong; it cannot triumph unless the Christian religion is a lie. Yet the converts to race segregation and subjection are growing alarmingly. We are today fighting for free common schools in Pennsylvania, for free ballots in Maryland, and for freedom of travel in the Nation. The cause of human freedom shrieks aloud in our every step. It is not because of our poverty, it is not because of our ignorance, it is not because of crime, it is not even because of race antipathy; it is simply the crude and bestial desire to oppress and abuse and murder wherever and whenever there is no fear of public opinion or courts of law or just retaliation. Once we were told: Be worthy and fit and the ways are open. Today the avenues of advancement in the army, navy and

From *The Horizon: A Journal of the Color Line* 4 (September 1908): 1–9.

civil service, and even in business and professional life, are continually closed to black applicants of proven fitness, simply on the bald excuse of race and color.

This is the spirit and practice which the Niagara Movement is fighting and will never cease to fight.

First: we say to our own: Obey the law, defend no crime, conceal no criminal, seek no quarrel: but arm yourselves, and when the mob invades your home, shoot, and shoot to kill.

Secondly: We say to voters: Register and vote whenever and wherever you have the right. Vote, not in the past, but in the present. Remember that the conduct of the Republican party toward Negroes has been a disgraceful failure to keep just promises. The dominant Roosevelt faction has sinned in this respect beyond forgiveness. We therefore trust that every black voter will uphold men like Joseph Benson Foraker, and will leave no stone unturned to defeat William H. Taft. Remember Brownsville, and establish next November the principle of independence in voting, not only for punishing enemies, but for rebuking false friends.

Let no bribe of money, office nor influence seduce the Negro American to betray the great principles of liberty, equality and opportunity. The race is not to the swift nor the battle to the strong. And the men today who think they can club ten million Negro Americans into inferiority and submission forget that God reigns and the Government at Washington still lives.

(Signed)

FREDERICK L. McGHEE, Minn.,
CHARLES E. BENTLEY, Ill.,
GERTRUDE W. MORGAN, Mass.,
WILLIAM E. HENDERSON, Ind.,
W. E. B. DuBois, Georgia.

THE NEGRO VOTE

Talk Number Four

THESIS: That the Democratic party deserves a trial at the hands of the Negro.

First a word as to the past:

The Democratic party has from the first been the party in American politics that believed in the widest participation of American citizens in the American government. This creed led to the overthrow of aristocratic tendencies in 1800, in 1828 and let us hope, in 1908. The enfranchisement of the common crowd brought, however, evils and temptations. Hesitation and war followed Jefferson, spoils and scandal followed Jackson, and an unholy alliance of democracy and slavery brought the Civil War.

Since the Civil War the impossible alliance of radical socialistic Democracy at the North with an aristocratic caste party at the South has been a spectacle for gods and men. The combination simply cannot last. The South does not believe in free trade and it does believe in Imperialism, caste-privilege and a free hand to corporate wealth. Why then is it linked with a party that stands for free trade, anti-imperialism, anti-caste and strict control of corporate wealth? Because it fears the Negro, and the Negro votes the Republican ticket blindly and solidly. Why does the Negro thus vote? Is it because he believes in high tariffs, the conquest of brown and black people and gently chastened Privilege? No, he believes in a low tariff, free Philippines and free labor. He votes against these things because he fears the South and the South is Democratic. Here then are two "solid" votes—great, unthinking, unreasoning wads of political power—voting against each other in blind hate and letting the country's interests and their own interests go to the devil.

Meantime the Democratic party faces a most exasperating *impasse*. Its most earnest professions of social uplift are negatived and contradicted by its Vardamans and Tillmans. And yet with the solid Negro vote against it, the Democratic party can only hope to win by aid of the Solid South.

The Negro voter today therefore has in his hand the tremendous power of emancipating the Democratic party from its enslavement to the reactionary South.

The Negro voter can deliver New York, New Jersey, Ohio, Indiana and Illinois to the Democrats with ease, and can make their triumph possible in a dozen other states. Do the Democrats want this aid? They do. Two out of three Democratic votes are cast in the North. There is not a single Northern state where the Democratic party has not offered every inducement to attract Negro voters. There is not a single Northern state where the Democrats have been in power, which has not treated Negroes better than the Republicans have. Who was it that slapped Tillman's impudent face in Chicago but a Democratic mayor? What Republican governor has approached the Democratic Johnson of Minnesota in consideration for this race? When were Negroes better treated than by President Cleveland?

What more do you ask, Mr. Black Voter? Do you expect the Democratic party to alienate the Solid South *before* it has any assurance of what you may do? Do you think it is a matter of pride to a decent, honest Northern Democrat to realize that only by condoning lies on Southern statute books can he get a chance to put liberal principles in power over this government? Do you imagine that he would not welcome the votes of honest men of any color in exchange for the dishonest votes that thrall him?

Why then does he not openly ask, sue and beg your vote? Because he doubts if you have sense enough to know your own good when you see it? Have you?

Then *vote for Bryan.*

Talk Number Five

Thesis: That the best thing that can happen in the next election will be a big black Bryan vote.

In November one of four things may happen:

1. Taft may win and receive the usual Negro vote.
2. Taft may win and receive only a part of the Negro vote.
3. Bryan may win by means of a part of the Negro vote.
4. Bryan may win without the aid of Negro votes.

Other possibilities are impossible. Without a large part of the Negro vote, Taft cannot possibly win and no third party has any chance.

Look at these results from the point of view of the Negro:

1. *If Taft gets the solid Negro vote and wins,* what then? The Negro has been brutally kicked; he has protested bitterly and then submissively tucking his tail

between his legs has obeyed his Master's voice. How much better off is he then than now?

2. But thanks be to God, Taft never can get the solid Negro vote. *If however Taft holds enough Negro votes to insure his election*, what then? Something will have been accomplished, but not much. If the warning is loud and the defection of Negro votes heavy, the Republicans may have sense enough to be careful in the future. They certainly will not repeat Brownsville. But the warning must be unmistakable.

3. *If Bryan wins, and wins by the aid of Negro votes*, what then? The Democratic party comes into power and knows that it can stay in power if it placates Negroes. The Republicans go out of power knowing that their outrageous treatment of Blacks caused their political downfall. Thereupon both parties will strive to deserve Negro votes, and this will be the beginning of Negro Freedom in this land.

4. *But if the Democratic party triumphs without the aid of Negro votes;* if after Roosevelt and Brownsville, Taft and Greensboro, the black voter crawls to his kennel rattling the same old chains while Democrats know they are under no obligations to the Negro vote—then *væ victis;* the hold of the Solid South will be strengthened and then good-bye to the 15th, if not to the 13th amendment. You don't believe it? Wait and see. Or, if you have too much sense to wait—*Vote for Bryan.*

A REPLY

To the Editor of the Horizon:

Will you permit me to take exception to your statement that "The cause of organized labor is the cause of black laborers?" A more correct statement would be that "The cause of non-union labor is the cause of black laborers." At the present time "organized labor" under the lead of such men as Gompers stands for monopoly and class rule—a monopoly just as despotic and injurious to the interests of the ordinary laborer as the monopoly of captial—a class rule just as vicious as the class rule of the Southern whites.

There is taking place in America at present a reaction against organized labor under its present leadership because of its tendency to establish a caste system and a despotic monopoly. There is a similar reaction against monopoly and Special Privilege on the part of capital.

The interests of colored laborers are opposed to monopoly, special privilege or caste systems in any form, they are therefore opposed to "organized labor."

The colored man should in all things stand for the recognition of individual merit without class distinction or special privilege. In politics that means civil service reform and the abolition of Jim Crow Car laws; in labor questions it means the "open shop," the cause of the independent workmen.

Very truly,

Boston, Mass.   Geo. G. Bradford.

22

The Over-Look

A betch o' bread thet han't riz once
ain't goin' to rise agin.
An' it's jest money throwed away to
put the empt'ins in.
J. R. Lowell.

BOOKS AND PERIODICALS

Since my last resume in the June HORIZON the following magazine articles worth reading have appeared:

July

Black Man, Silent Power of the. Ray S. Baker. AMERICAN.
Fifteenth Amendment, Repeal of. T. B. Edgington. NORTH AMERICAN.
Indians Past and Present, Some. A. W. Dimock. OUTING.
Jew, The, and the Currents of his Age. A. S. Isaacs. ATLANTIC.
Lincoln and Darwin, Centennial of. W. R. Thayer. NORTH AMERICAN.
Negro Co-operative Society, A. By R. L. Smith. WORLD'S WORK.
Southern Race Question, Outcome of. A. B. Hart. N. AMERICAN.

August

Indian Compound, Life in an. Mary A. Chamberlain. ATLANTIC.
Negro, Voodoo and the. Marvin Dana. METROPOLITAN.
Negroes, Agricultural Extension among the. WORLD TODAY.
Philippine Assembly, The. By J. A. LeRoy. WORLD TODAY.
Southern Statesmanship, The New. By Ray S. Baker. AMERICAN.
"Uncle Remus," The Author of. REVIEW OF REVIEWS.

September

Mindanao and Sulu, Our Constabulary in. WORLD TODAY.
Negro, What to do about the. By Ray S. Baker. AMERICAN.
White Race in the Tropics, The. S. P. Verner. WORLD'S WORK.
Why the Difference? Negro crimes in Portsmouth, Va. and Springfield. W. A. Woodridge.
INDEPENDENT, 65: 605–6.

From *The Horizon: A Journal of the Color Line* 4 (October 1908): 1–8.

Blame for the Riot at Springfield. NATION, 87: 284.
Race War in the North. By W. E. Walling. INDEPENDENT, 65: 529–34.†
So-called Race Riot at Springfield. CHARITIES, 20: 709–11.
Convict Lease System of Georgia. A. J. Kelway. OUTLOOK, 90: 67–72.

October

American Black; poem. G. H. Clarke. FORUM, 40:346–7.
Negro Governments in the North. REVIEW OF REVIEWS, 38: 471–2.
Turkey in Europe; history laboratory. W. M. Sloane. POL. SCI. QUARTERLY, 23: 297–319.
Welding the Races. H. Bumstead. OUTLOOK, 90: 46–7.

The books published since June, which are of more or less interest to us are:

The Causes of the Present Discontent in India. By C. J. O'Donnell. 8vo, pp 120. A. Wessels Co. 85 cents net.
African Nature Notes and Reminiscences. By Frederick Courtney Selous: with a "Foreword" by President Roosevelt. Illus., 8vo, gilt top, pp 356. Macmillan Co. $3.00 net.
South Africa at Home. By Robert Fuller, Illus. 12mo, pp 236. Chas Scribner's Sons. $1.75 net.
Pleasure and Problem in South Africa. By Cecil Harmsworth. Illus. 12mo, gilt top, pp 252. Jno. Lane Co. $1.50 net.
Race or Mongrel. By Alfred P. Schultz. 12mo, gilt top, uncut, pp 369. L. C. Page & Co. $2.50.
Studies in the American Race Problem. By Alfred Holt Stone, with introduction and three papers by Walter F. Wilcox. 8vo, gilt top, uncut, pp 555. Doubleday Page & Co. $3.00 net.

100–21 = 79

We have to date twenty-one guarantors, who pledge themselves for one year to pay $500.00 toward the support of the enlarged Horizon, viz:

1. F. H. M. MURRAY, Alexandria, Va.
2. L. M. HERSHAW, Washington, D. C.
3. W. E. B. DuBOIS, Atlanta, Ga.
4. F. L. McGHEE, St. Paul, Minn.
5. JOSEPH SHERWOOD, St. Paul, Minn.
6. L. R. DIGGS, Frankfort, Ky.
7. C. E. BENTLEY, Chicago, Ill.
8. E. C. WILLIAMS, Cleveland, Ohio
9. Anonymous, No. 1, Atlanta, Ga.
10. Anonymous, No. 2, Washington, D. C.
11. MURRAY BROTHERS, Washington, D. C.
12. DR. HENRY L. BAILEY, Washington, D. C.
13. Anonymous, No. 3, New York, N.Y.

14. Geo. W. MITCHELL, Philadelphia, Pa.
15. Anonymous, No. 4, Cincinnati, O.
16. G. W. CRAWFORD, New Haven, Conn.
17. Dr. S. C. FULLER, [*] Westborough, Mass.
18. W. A. HAWKINS, Baltimore, Md.
19. Anonymous, No. 5, [*] Washington, D. C.
20. THOS A. JOHNSON, Washington, D. C.
21. Rev. J. MILTON WALDRON, Wash., D. C.

[* partial]

Eight others have indicated that they probably will help, making in sight 29 guarantors and a fund of $700.00. The success thus far and the reasonable certainty of securing a guarantee fund of $1,250, if not the total amount asked for, makes it possible to announce that the enlarged and reorganized Horizon will begin publication with Volume V. No. I, on January Ist, 1909. It will be (subject to the direction of the guarantors who will own it) a magazine with at least thrice the present amount of reading matter, and having among other features, correspondents' letters, a careful digest of news concerning the darker races the world over, book and magazine news, a review of the Negro Press, and editorial comment. The Horizon will still aim at quality rather than quantity, and it will maintain the frank freedom of its opinions.

While the guarantee fund is sufficiently large to warrant this prospectus, it is not yet of nearly sufficient size. We need seventy-nine more men to come forward and promise to pay at their convenience during the coming year 1909, twenty-five dollars for the purpose of maintaining a dignified unfettered monthly magazine representing the best thought of this race.

We would prefer to publish the names of all donors, but this is not possible in all cases, as the following letter shows:

......, Oct. 16, 1908

Dear Dr. DuBois:—

I regret to say that I must resign from membership in the Niagara Movement for the reason that I am about to begin work in ...... I should be glad to send you a secret subscription to the able periodical with which you are connected, but I have not the money. Speaking of secret subscriptions, let me say that they are absolutely necessary to the cause. There are many who dare not for good reasons speak or contribute openly who ought to know of the method of rendering substantial aid to a cause which, I am sure, lies close to really all Negroes' and many white men's hearts. All praise to those who dare speak and act openly, but let us be considerate of those who would speak and act openly if they dared. The thing to insist on is that no man says he believes something he does not believe and contributes to a cause he disbelieves in. Let there be silence and inaction in such matters.

I may later find it possible to be associated with you openly but for the present my resignation is final. You shall have a secret comrade in me. My private prayers shall go up for you who dare, and when opportunity affords I shall be a secret subscriber to our common cause.

Yours for the Cause,

(signed)

THE NEGRO VOTE

Talk Number Six

When this reaches many of our readers' eyes the deed will be almost if not quite done, and the next president of the United States almost if not quite chose. Whoever he is we welcome him to a tremendous task. The task, *first*, of curbing the vicious power of corporate wealth; the task, *second*, of enforcing law and order in this lawless land. And *last*—and in the bitterness of our extremity we think not least but greatest—the task of securing to Negro Americans their full rights of American citizens lest race prejudice undermine the walls of our nation's liberty.

This is your task Mr. President and you cannot shirk. You owe your election to Negro votes. To the belief of the majority of 200,000 black men that you are brave and patriotic enought to be a MAN and not merely a white man. Will you justify this faith so generously expressed or will you follow the footsteps of Theodore Roosevelt? From such a fate God save us all.

"In the Transvaal and other self-governing colonies the proportion of natives satisfying the requirements of the Cape franchise is so small, and will probably for many years to come continue so small, that, even with the manhood suffrage established in the Transvaal "the black vote" could not be attended by any of the dangers which alarmed the South African Native Affairs Commission; but the proposed concession would be an act of justice, and an earnest of good faith, of the highest value in conciliating and befriending the uncivilized as well as the civilized natives. To the uncivilized natives, moreover, no less welcome and serviceable would be the adoption of the policy, identical in principle though diverse in the details of its application, which was recommended by both the Johannesburg and the Pietermaritzburg Native Affairs Commissions, and which has been favoured by Lord Selborne in Basutoland and Swaziland. If the uncivilized natives in each of the large areas occupied by them were allowed to send one or more direct representatives either to separate Councils for Native Affairs or to the Colonial Parliaments in which questions affecting their interests would be discussed—in the latter case, perhaps, only with advisory, and not voting powers—notable preparation would be made for the steady development of an ideal South Africa, in which the white and the black inhabitants of the country would be able to work in harmony for the welfare of the whole community. One advantage of the suggested arrangement would be, it may be expected, that no friction need arise in a gradual transition from the present disorganized and troubled condition of affairs to the state of order and prosperity which is now being ostensibly aimed at by all sections of the white population."

—*The Aborigines' Friend.*

From Abroad

Port Limon, Costa Rica, C. A.
October 25, 1908.

Dear Dr. DuBois:

I have not received "The Horizon" since. . . . I am sorry for this for we miss the magazine very much. It is one of those we cannot do without.

Yours sincerely,
WM. FORDE.

EDITOR'S NOTE

†Du Bois calls attention to three articles about the pogrom that ravaged Springfield, Illinois, during July 1908, when two Black men were lynched, four white men were killed, and over 70 people were injured. In particular, the article by William English Walling helped bring about the events that led to the founding of the N.A.A.C.P.

23

The Over-Look

POLITICS

I have noticed with a great deal of interest the attitude of the various Negro publications on the outcome of the Presidential election. The greater number of these publications have tacitly or openly recognized that the election of Mr. Taft by a overwhelming majority was a great blow to the Negro people. Those who wished his election felt the blow because they knew that he was elected without the help of the Negro vote. To those who did not wish his election it was a blow because they were not able to hold the usual balance of power.

Without doubt more Negroes voted against Mr. Taft than ever before voted against a Republican Candidate. Other considerations, however, and especially the unfortunate attitude of the Labor vote, defeated Mr. Bryan. It is to be hoped that the outcome will not be as unfortunate for the Negro as is certainly possible. Mr. Taft's speech before the North Carolina Society in New York is re-assuring; it is by far the best thing that he has said, and if it were the only thing that he had said or done it would be entirely satisfactory. At the same time the Negro knows that the Lily White Movement in the South is menacing, and that Mr. Taft has, up until the present, stood behind and encouraged that movement. The Negro knows that the last decision of the Supreme Court is one of the worst decisions for human rights which that unfortunate court ever made.† With these two things staring them in the face, nevertheless the race goes forward, but it should go forward with this distinctly in mind: Political organization on racial lines must be kept up. We did not happen to have the power in the last election of deciding who should be President but we will have the power in certain future elections. We should be able so far as possible to count our vote substantially as a unit, and to cast it for those people who are going to stand for human rights. The Political League, therefore, under Mr. Waldron, should be kept organized. Mr. Waldron has also accepted the chairman-ship of the Suffrage department of the Niagara Movement, which will for practical purposes unite the efforts of these two organizations. We should be ready in the next two years to dictate the election or the retirement of certain congressmen, and four years from today we should stand ready to make Mr. Taft give an account of his stewardship: to re-elect him, if he has done well; to seek by all legitimate means to defeat him if he does ill.

From *The Horizon: A Journal of the Color Line* 4 (November/December 1908): 11–14.

LIBERIA

The full significance of the recent visit of Liberian envoys to the United States has not perhaps been appreciated. Liberia needs capital and skilled economic direction. Today, however, capital and political control tend to go hand in hand. Today it is English capital and English skill which is developing Liberia. This is dangerous to the Independence of the Liberian State. Consequently a young Liberian party has arisen, who wish to displace English capital and English influence with American capital and enterprise. This younger element after great struggle succeeded in getting a special embassy sent to the United States for the discussion of these matters. It is unfortunate that these envoys could not have been more fittingly received and more definitely, reassured, but that was our fault as Negro-Americans and not theirs.

The whole transaction illustrates the need of greater solidarity, knowledge and co-operation among men of Negro descent. We must have a second and greater Pan-African movement, and the time to inaugurate it is on the Jubilee of American Emancipation in 1913. The cause of Liberia, the cause of Haiti, the cause of South Africa is our cause, and the sooner we realize this the better.

THE NEW HORIZON

With the January number the new Horizon will begin.‡ Each number will be published on or about the fifteenth of the month, and we shall try to be prompt. The size of the new Horizon will be about six by nine inches, thirty-two pages and illustrated. It will have the following departments:

Editorials
A Digest of News
A Digest of Opinion
A Review of the Negro Press
A Woman's Department
Book News
A Contributed Article

Such a publication will involve, of course, largely increased expense. We wish to begin the new Horizon with a subscription list of at least five hundred and we hope before the end of the year that this may reach two thousand; whether it will or not depends upon our friends. The price of the new Horizon will be one dollar. If each of our present subscribers will try to get us two or three subscribers it will be possible to make the Horizon, in time, a permanent institution. Otherwise the experiment will be confined simply to the year 1909.

EDITOR'S NOTES
†The reference is to *Berea College v. Kentucky,* 211 U.S., 26 (1908); the Supreme Court held that a state could prohibit, under the separate-but-equal doctrine, even a *private* college from instructing whites and Blacks together.

‡As noted in the Introduction, Du Bois's hopes were not realized; an expanded *Horizon* did not appear until November 1909.

24

The Over-Look

OUR POLICY

THIS IS A RADICAL PAPER. It stands for progress and advance. It advocates Negro equality and human equality; it stands for Universal suffrage, including votes for Women; it believes in the abolition of War, the taxation of monopoly values, the gradual socialization of capital and the overthrow of persecution and dogmatism in the name of religion. At the same time our policy is grounded in common-sense: it does not seek to force human brotherhood by act of legislature, it does not regard voting as a panacea for all ills; it honors marriage and motherhood, upholds the sometime piteous necessity of righteous self-defense, believes and maintains that what a man earns is his, and believes always in Good and God.

SUPPORT

If you believe in these things, Reader, and want them honestly and fearlessly, but always decently, advocated, then we want you to support this enterprise by contributing to it from time to time such sums as you can spare. No periodical that advocates unpopular or partially popular causes can be a self-supporting business proposition. A modern magazine gets its support from advertisements. Paying revenue of that sort cannot be expected for such a monthly as this. We must depend upon subscriptions and donations—subscriptions from all who subscribe to our creed, and donations to enable us to convert the Heathen. It is just as reasonable to pay the expenses of an organ to disseminate your views as it is to contribute to church or lodge, or mission work of any kind.

NATIONAL NEGRO CONFERENCE

The most significant event of 1909 was the meeting of the National Negro Conference in New York last May. Hitherto there has been in this country a strange, to some, almost inexplicable hiatus between the cause of Negro uplift and other great causes of human advance. If one met the workers for women's rights, prison reform, improvement in housing, consumer's leagues, social settlements, universal peace, socialism, almost any of the myriad causes for which thinkers and doers are today toiling, one met persons who usually either knew nothing of the Negro problem or avoided it if they did know. On the other hand Negroes have long been working on the theory that the Negro problem is separate and distinct from other social problems in America, and to be settled by peculiar remedies. Today both sets

From *The Horizon: A Journal of the Color Line* 5 (November 1909): 1–2, 8–9.

of social workers are awakened to their mistake, and the New York Conference is the first fruits of that awakening. Social workers who called that conference, like Jane Addams, Anna Carlin Spencer, Florence Kelley, Oswald Garrison Villard, Charles Edward Russell, Lillian D. Wald, William English Walling and others are today realizing that there is in America today no human problem of advance and uplift which does not in a more or less subtle way involve the Negro American and his condition, and that so long as he is systematically degraded, degradation will be the portion of large numbers of his fellow white citizens. So too, the Negroes who responded eagerly to the call are beginning to learn that the Negro problem is simply a problem of poverty, ignorance, suffrage, women's rights, distribution of wealth, and law and order among both blacks and whites, and that to attack any of these evils properly involves close cooperation with the great reform forces of the day. The Negro problem is not simply a matter of millionaires and almsgiving— it is a human problem and demands human methods. It is to be sincerely hoped that the committee of forty appointed by the Conference will draft a comprehensive permanent organization embracing the workers for reform in all lines for the special object of uplifting the black American.

GARRISON

In the death of William Lloyd Garrison the younger, the Negro race loses a staunch and courageous friend. Indeed, bearing the name he did, he could scarce have been less. He was however a peculiar example of one who shed lustre on an historic name. This he did not so much by burning a brighter flame, but a different one. He approached the same problem that interested the father in a different way, with his own methods, and yet helped and illuminated them. One could not sit there in Park Street Church at his memorial, without continual wonder at the catholicity of this many sided, yet sweet and simple soul. The Woman said: "He never talked down to us," and not a black man there but knew the fineness of this eulogy: the Minister spoke of the man who "Never cast side-glances to see what was to become of himself or of his personal interest." The brave socialist Editor of Chicago said that Garrison believed that "Righteousness was the only permissible form of expediency," and the Artist spoke of his sympathizing love. It is a great thing to have a Father. It is greater to have a Son.

HENSON

There is a strange fatality about America and the Negro. One can part them neither in thought or fact. From the day Stephen Dorantes first looked on the great Southwest to year 1909 when Mathew Henson stood with Peary at the North Pole, the Negro has shared nearly every great American deed or event. The superficial sneer at the manner of much of this sharing: Henson was but a servant they say; Estevanico was a slave. True Henson was but a servant, and so was Jesus Christ, and until we recognize the true glory of service in America we shall have our servant problem. Henson was a servant but not a hireling. He was hired not by the week but for life. For long hard dreary years he has held up the hands of a man fighting to conquer nature in her grimmest fastness. He was serving neither for honor nor wealth but by reason of his devotion to a human being and that being's dream.

What he did his race has done and ever will do—the truest, finest exponents of love and tenderness, of single-hearted faith, in a contemptible age of bull dogs, Big Sticks and Lion slaughterers.

SCHOOLS

Let us not forget the school children in these days of beginning the World's year's work. In this autumnal season seventeen million children have entered the doors of the public schools and of these over three million are colored.

The facilities open to these children in the South are meagre. The rural Negro public school is, save in a few localities, worse than ten years ago. The public Negro High Schools in the South have in a single year been cut from the ridiculously small number of 121 with an enrollment of 7067, to 106 enrolling 6860.

Only 55 per cent of the colored youth between five and eighteen years of age are enrolled in school and only two-thirds of these regularly attend the short terms provided. The South for the most part is making quiet but sustained and strenuous efforts to stop Negro education while we are sitting around trying to get some worthless politician a new job at Washington.

———

The third biennial session of the Congregational Workers among Colored People was held at Birmingham, Ala., Sept. 15, 1909.

———

The Colored Branch of the Louisville Public Library cost $41,609.02. Its circulation:

1st year	17,838
2nd year	30,259
3rd year	35,910
4th (9 months)	39,754

It has 6882 volumes, and 65 periodicals.

BOOKS

The Negro Problem, Abraham Lincoln's Solution, by William P. Pickett. Putnams', Philadelphia, 1909, 580 pp. 8vo.

Chords and Discords, by Walter Everett Hawkins. Murray Bros., Washington, 1909, 81 pp. 12mo.

The Upward Path, The Evolution of a Race, by Mary Helm; Young People's Missionary Movement, etc., 1909, 333 pp. 8vo.

The Negro American Family, edited by W. E. Burghardt Du Bois. Atlanta, University Press, 1908, 156 pp. 8vo.

Self Help in Negro Education, by R. R. Wright, Jr. (Philadelphia).

Public Taxation and Negro Schools, pamphlet, Committee of Twelve, Cheney, Pa., 1909.

Journal, National Medical Association, (quarterly). Vol. I, Nos. 1, 2 and 3. C. V. Roman, editor-in-chief.

The Negro Question, by Eberhard Haven. Baltimore, 22 pp. 1908.

Some Phases of the Negro Question, by C. W. Melick. Mt. Rainer, Md., 1908, 91 pp.

———

The 13th Annual Report of the Hampton Negro Conference contains 63 pages as follows:

The Modern Idea of Education, by H. B. Frissell.
Hookworm Disease and the Negroes, by C. W. Stiles.
Negro Anti-tuberculosis Leagues, by C. P. Wertenbaker.
Community Work of Colored Schools, by W. T. B. Williams.
Negro Life Insurance, by W. S. Dodd.
Farm Demonstration Work, by J. B. Pierce.
Crime among Negroes, by Kelly Miller.
Crime among Negroes, by J. F. Hewins.
The Work of the Minister, A. A. Graham.

———

Mr. William P. Pickett has published a thick volume advocating the assisted *Emigration of American Negroes to Africa.* The tone of the work is not good, the facts are inaccurate and the logic strained. It seems a pity that any well-intentioned man should waste so much time and money. The Negro Problem is to be settled here in America and settled right. After that we shall be ready and willing to help our brothers in Africa. To jump however, now from the frying pan to the fire is an experiment which we can scarcely be induced to try.

PERIODICALS

Africa in Transformation, by C. C. Adams. Review of Reviews, March, 1909.
Africa that Roosevelt will see, by C. B. Taylor. Everybody's, March, 1909.
Africa: Where Roosevelt will Go, by T. R. MacMechan. McClure's, March, 1909.
Africa's Native Problem, by Olive Schreiner. Review of Reviews, March, 1909.
Home Rule in Cuba, by C. N. de Dutland. World To–day, March, 1909.
Heart of Negro Problem, by Quincy Ewing. Atlantic, March, 1909.
Hunting in East Africa, by P. C. Madera. Metropolitan, May, 1909.
The Hunter's Paradise, East Africa, by D. A. Wiley. Putnams', May, 1909.
Savings of Georgia Negroes, by W. E. B. DuBois. World's Work, May, 1909.
Southern Problems, by Harrison. Everybody's, May, 1909.
Cuba's Future, by H. A. Austin. North American, June, 1909.
The Unknowable Negro, by Harris Dickson. Hampton's, June, 1909.
White Slaves in Africa, by T. W. Higginson. North American, July 1909.
Black and White in the South, by W. Archer. McClure's, July, 1909.
African Game Trails, by Theodore Roosevelt. Scribner's, October, 1909.
Long in Darke, by W. E. B. DuBois. Independent, October 21, 1909.
Into Africa with Roosevelt, by E. B. Clark. Review of Reviews, March, 1909.

ALONG THE COLOR LINE

Niagara Movement

The Fifth Annual Address of the Niagara Movement deserves wide reading:

For four years the Niagara Movement has struggled to make ten million Americans of Negro descent cease from mere apology and weak surrender to aggression, and take a firm unfaltering stand for justice, manhood and self-assertion. We are accumulating property at a constantly accelerating rate; we are rapidly lowering our rate of illiteracy; but property and intelligence are of little use unless guided by the great ideals of Freedom, Justice and Human Brotherhood.

As a partial result of our effort we are glad to note among us increasing spiritual unrest, sterner impatience with cowardice and deeper determination to be men at any cost.

Along with undoubted advance and development within, there continues without unceasing effort to discourage and proscribe us. We not only travel in public ignominy and discomfort, but at the instance of some of our weak kneed leaders, the Inter-State Commerce Commission has recently sought to make a pitiful apology for this disgrace.

Our right to work is questioned not only by some who are attempting to fight the great battles of labor, but even by these very people who declare us fit for nothing else.

We are glibly told to deserve before we complain; yet those of us who do deserve are proscribed along with the least by men who know that ability and desert come oftenest through freedom and power. Such power we must have: Political power, Economic power, power of Mind.

We had enough political power to rebuke the President who blundered at Brownsville and was too stubborn to say so; we still have enough power to rebuke the President who proposes to turn competent black men out of all positions which any white man wants. We have this power now but unless we use it we shall lose it. Our organized enemies seek to scare and villify us while they despoil us. We have fewer criminals than our systematic training in crime warrants; yet we are daily pictured as thugs and murderers and lynched without trial for the crime of any scamp who blacks his face.

Peonage and prejudice are used to keep our wages low and education is proposed to fit us only for menial service.

Do men forget that the wages of white Americans cannot permanently rise far above the wages of black Americans, and do they not know that the half-drunken senator who can today slap a black laborer's face may tomorrow kick white laborers down stairs? And yet who too often lead the fight against us? Poor and ignorant whites, spurred on by the richer and more intelligent who hide behind the mob and fatten on its deeds. Small wonder that Negro disfranchisement is practically coincident with those regions where white ignorance, political fraud and murder are greatest.

That black men are inherently inferior to white men is a wide-spread lie which science flatly contradicts, and the attempt to submerge the colored races is one with world-old efforts of the wily to exploit the weak. We must therefore make common cause with the oppressed and down-trodden of all races and peoples; with our kindred of South Africa and West Indies; with our fellows in Mexico, India and Russia and with the cause of working classes everywhere.

On us rests to no little degree the burden of the cause of individual Freedom, Human Brotherhood, and Universal Peace in a day when America is forgetting her promise and destiny. Let us work on and never despair because pigmy voices are loudly praising ill-gotten wealth, big guns and human degradation. They but represent back eddies in the Tide of Time. The causes of God cannot be lost.

25

The Over-Look

JOHN BROWN AND CHRISTMAS

This is Christmas time and the time of John Brown. On the second of this month he was crucified, on the 8th he was buried and on the 25th, fifty years later let him rise from the dead in every Negro-American home. Jesus Christ came not to bring peace but a sword. So did John Brown. Jesus Christ gave his life as a sacrifice for the lowly. So did John Brown. Both these mighty spirits were failures: they owned no real estate, had no money, kept no bank accounts and received no homage. Of both these souls it was said and still is said:

"He is despised and rejected of men; a man of sorrows, and acquainted with grief: and we hid as it were our faces from him; he was despised, and we esteemed him not.

"Surely he hath borne our griefs, and carried our sorrows; yet we did esteem him stricken, smitten of God, and afflicted.

"But he was wounded for our transgressions, he was bruised for our iniquities; the chastisement of our peace was upon him; and with his stripes we are healed.

"All we like sheep have gone astray; we have turned every one to his own way; and the Lord hath laid on him the iniquity of us all."

THE COLOR LINE

After you draw the Color Line where have you drawn it? You never know. The Constitution of the New South African Union confines voting to "persons of European descent." What does that mean? No one knows. Does it include the Hon. H. C. Hull, Treasurer of the Transvaal? Everybody knows that both Dr. Hull and his wife are mulattoes or quadroons. Does it include the 500,000 "colored" people of Cape Colony? Does it include the thousands of Boers who have Negro blood? No one knows.

WOMEN

The signs of awakening womanhood in the world to-day are legion. The best novelists are women. Some of the keenest essayists and graceful writers of verse are women. Women are among the greatest leaders of Social Reforms, and at last in England they are fighting, literally fighting, for their political rights. Of course there are fools a plenty to tell them they don't need the ballot and to feed them the ancient taffy about homes and babies. How natural it is that the *Outlook* of the

From *The Horizon: A Journal of the Color Line* 5 (December 1909): 1, 2–3, 10, 11–12.

Philistines should with one hand rub the "nigger's" nose in the dirt and with the other slap women into prositution, the while piously rolling its eyes to God and increasing its circulation. But this is the second forward coming of the women and beneath it is a ground swell that none can long resist. The second forward coming of black men is not far off when the hypnotism of present bribery and ring rule falls.

GENERAL HOWARD

General Howard was a singular psychological study. Of his perfect sincerity none could doubt. His sacrifices for the causes he loved, among them that of the Negro in America, were great and on the whole effective. Yet he fell short of the world's expectations in many ways, chiefly because such tremendous responsibilities were thrust upon him. If he had been a world genius his opportunity to serve mankind would have been the greatest of the 19th century. Think of the chance of dictating the fortunes of four million freedmen and their employers after a social cataclysm: suppose the tremendous experiment of Freedmen's Bureau had been, not a partial, but a conspicuous success? To be sure such success demanded almost superhuman power and Howard was very human, weakly human. He felt his weakness and became, therefore, intensely religious with an orthodoxy altogether too simple and childlike to be true. He is gone. The Negro race mourns a friend and benefactor and the nation mourns an honest man, whose honor is that he always tried to do his whole duty and whose only fault, if fault it could be called, was a natural capacity that fell far short of his opportunities.

MR. TAFT

Every time a man begins to sacrifice principles in order to curry favor with people who know they are wrong, he essays a thankless task. The distance between right and wrong is infinite, but the step from one wrong to more wrong is slight and this all mischievous men know and emphasize. Mr. Taft has promised the South an unfair thing which flatly contradicts every tried rule of civil service: viz., to appoint men to office not because of their fitness for the duties of the office but in accordance with the personal prejudices of a part of their neighbors, even when those prejudices are the least defensible among civilized men. In South Carolina where most men are black, the *News and Courier* rejoices over six new appointments all *"white* men" and mostly "Democrats." Yet is the South satisfied? No sirree! Mr. F. D. Winston of North Carolina calmly slaps the President's other cheek and kicks him. He tells him to mind his own business and announces that the South is enraged over the one unequivocal thing which Mr. Taft has said on the race problem—the Maryland letter.

Facilis descensus Averno, sed—.

CONSISTENCY

Listen to Bernard Shaw's defense of Hall Caine's "White Prophet":
"It is lucky for the officials that the English are not logical; for the first half of the official story is that the Egyptians are such abject slaves and cowards that England

had to rescue them from the most horrible oppression by Ismail, and could make soldiers of them only by giving them English officers; and the second half is that they are so desperately ferocious, bloody-minded and implacable, that at a word of encouragement from an English novelist, they will rise and sweep the Occupation into the Nile after ravishing all the white women and massacring all the white men. But nobody sees the incoherence. As the first half shows the Englishman as magnificently superior, and the second as dauntlessly brave, he does not notice that they flatly contradict one another."

Does not this sound strangely familiar? The Negroes of the South are such "abject slaves and cowards" they can make no progress save under white leadership and tutelage which shows the Southern white "magnificently superior." Also the Negroes are so "desperate, ferocious, bloody-minded and implacable" that unless Mr. Taft pardons the lyncher of Chattanooga all white women are lost. Which shows the "dauntless bravery" of them that keep the Negroes down!

A CORRESPONDENCE

From a white professor in a Southern University:
Prof. W. E. B. DuBois,
    Atlanta University.
Dear Sir:—
    I have just read the tragedy which you call "The Souls of Black Folk," and I cannot refrain from writing to tell you how profoundly it has affected me. It is faint praise—but even the pure English was very refreshing in this day of slovenliness.
    The pathetic part of the whole thing is what you stress repeatedly—that the control of the South is not in the hands of its best people. The problem is the problem of the lower class whites, and the more enlightened are utterly powerless. I have long grieved over your own position, and wished that there could be some alleviation, and known that there could be none. I have, however, wanted you to know that my skirts at least are clean. I have never wittingly wronged one of your race in any way. I have never defrauded one of them of money, I have never insulted one of them. I have been careful to train my children to respect their feelings in every way, and have punished them for offenses in this respect which I should also have passed over. And I have been able to be of service to many of them in more ways than in the matter of money. The principal of the city schools here has had regular teaching from me in both Latin and German, and I have been able also to help others. Of course I voted against disfranchisement.
    This is a very small thing, but your book has put me on the defensive . These things I have done and left undone, and yet my whole training and environment have been such that I cannot break away from the other things of which you complain—I should not use the word, because the book is notably free from complaint. You, in turn, must look as leniently as you can on feelings which have been made part of us, and we must labor together, in all ways, to lighten the gloom. And with it all rest assured that many of us feel most deeply the pathos of your own position.
                        Yours very truly, _____

The answer:

My dear Sir:

I have read your very kindly letter again and again with increasing interest and sympathy. I have taken the liberty to read it to some of my friends and they have been both moved and encouraged. I thank you for your frank words and I want to say two things in answer to them which I trust will not sound ungracious. First, whenever an aristocracy allows a mob to rule the fault is not with the mob; and secondly, Comrade, you and I can never be satisfied with sitting down before a great human problem and saying nothing can be done. We must do something. That is the reason we are on Earth.

Again thanking you for your kind words, I beg to remain

Very sincerely yours,

W. E. B. DuBois

BOOKS & PERIODICALS

During the year 1909 ninety-eight separate pieces of literature treated of the Negro-American. Of these twenty were books. Of the books four are of unusual interest, viz:

Southern South, by A. B. Hart. $1.50, Appleton.
Basis of Ascendency, by E. G. Murphy. $1.50, Longmans.
Christian Reconstruction in the South, by H. P. Douglass. $1.50, Pilgrim press.
Southerner, by N. Worth. $1.20, Doubleday.

Of the other books two are reprints of former editions. The other fourteen are:

Solid South and the Afro-American race problem, by C. F. Adams, Jr., 23 Court Street, Boston.
Spirit of the South, by W. W. Harney. $1.50, R. G. Badger.
Grant Vernon: a Boston boy's adventures in Louisiana, by E. B. Stanton. $1.00, Roxburgh pub.
South in the building of the nation. 12v, $60, Southern hist. pub. soc., Richmond, Va.
Negro American Family, W. E. B. Du Bois, ed., Pa. 75¢, Atlanta University press, Atlanta, Ga.
Upward Path: the evolution of a race, by M. Helm. 50¢, Young People's Missionary Movement.
Seeking the best: dedicated to the Negro youth, by O. M. Shackelford. $1.00, Hudson.
Virginia's attitude toward slavery and secession, by B. B. Munford. $2.00, Longmans.
John Brown, by W. E. B. Du Bois. $1.25, Jacobs.
Black Bishop, by Crowther, Samuel Adjal, J. Page. $2.00, Revell.
Dred Scott case, by E. W. R. Ewing. Legal and historical status of the Dred Scott decision. $3, Cobden pub. co., Washington, D. C.
Negro problem: Abraham Lincoln's solution, by W. P. Pickett. $2.50, Putnam.
Out of the darkness, by J. W. Grant, $1.10, National Bapt.
Bright side of Memphis, by G. P. Hamilton. $2.50 Memphis, Tenn.

There were fifteen pamphlets of importance published. Two of these are notable:

Public taxation and Negro schools, by C. L. Coon, Cheyney, Pa.
Self help in Negro education, by R. R. Wright, Cheyney, Pa.

The other thirteen are:

Needs of the South, by S. E. Griggs. Pa. 10¢, Orion pub. co.
South and Mr. Taft, by Silas McBee. New York.
Our inheritance, by A. Withers. 50¢, Elmhurst, Cal.
Conference for education in the South. Proceedings of the twelfth conference, New York.
Negro problem (Bibliography), R. H. Edwards. ed. Pa. 10¢, Madison, Wis.
Separate or "Jim Crow" car laws, by R. H. Boyd. Pa. 25¢, National Bapt.
Race question in a new light by S. E. Griggs. Pa. 15¢, National Bapt.
Equality of rights for all citizens, black and white alike, by F. J. Grimke. 15¢, Washington, D. C.
Progress and development of the colored people of our nation, by F. J. Grimke. 10¢, Washington, D. C.
From Darkness to light: the story of Negro progress, by M. Helm. 50¢, Pa. 30¢, Revell.
Ideas on education, by S. C. Armstrong. Hampton, Va.

There have been as far as the available records go sixty-three articles in the larger national periodicals as follows:

Outlook	*18*
Nation	*8*
Independent	*7*
World's Work	*5*
Annals of the American Academy	*4*
Survey	*3*
Harper's Weekly	*3*
Atlantic	*2*
Spirit of Missions	*2*
McClure's	*2*
Hampton's	*2*
Review of Reviews	*1*
Political Science Quarterly	*1*
American Magazine	*1*
Delineator	*1*

Twenty-one of these articles were editorial or staff writers' comments. Ten others were signed by Mr. Booker T. Washington. Three articles were by Harris Dickson, a Mississippi white lawyer, three were by W. E. B. Du Bois, and two by M. N. Work. Only four colored writers' names appear. This of course takes no account of church papers, and distinctively Negro periodicals.

The five most notable articles were:

Black and white in the South, by W. Archer. *McClure,* July.
Heart of the race problem, by Q. Ewing. *Atlantic,* March.
Race problems in America, by F. Boas. *Science,* May 28.
Ultimate race problem, by K. Miller. *Atlantic,* April.
Conflict of color: the World to-day and how color divides it, by L. P. Weale. *World's Work,* September.

The others are:

Achievements of Negroes, by B. T. Washington. *Independent,* September 30.
Free Negro in slavery days, by B. T. Washington. *Outlook,* September 18.
Law and order and the Negro, by B. T. Washington. *Outlook,* November 6.
Long in Darke, by W. E. B. DuBois. *Independent,* October 21.
Negro disfranchisement and the Negro in business, by B. T. Washington. *Outlook,* October 9.
Negro in a democracy, by R. S. Baker. *Independent,* September 9.
Vampire of the South, by M. H. Carter. *McClure,* September 18.
Brownsville again. *Outlook,* December 26, 1908.
Exit Brownsville. *Outlook,* March 6.
Commencement at Hampton, by a Spectator. *Outlook,* May 15.
Negro races, by J. Dowd. Review. *Political Science Quarterly,* December, 1908.
Who pays the Negroes' school bill. *World Work,* July.
Negro in Africa and America. *Outlook,* May 29.
Story of the Negro, by B. T. Washington. *Outlook,* September 4.
Aunt 'Liza, one of the slaves who stayed, by L. Finch. *American Magazine,* February.
Breaking away of mammy: story, by V. F. Doyle. *Delineator,* February.
Definite progress among Negroes, *Outlook,* July 31.
Liberty, equality and fraternity limited, *Independent,* June 10.
Lincoln and the Negro, by M. P. Andrews. *Nation,* March 18. *World's Work,* April.
National committee on the Negro, by W. E. B. Du Bois. *Survey,* June 12.

Negro mine laborer; central Appalachian coal field, by G. T. Surface. *Annals of the American Academy*, March.

Race prejudice by E. L. C. Morse. *Nation*, March 17.

Science and human brotherhood, by W. E. Walling. *Independent*, June 17.

Science of race-hatred. *Nation*, July 8.

Berean school of Philadelphia and the industrial efficiency of the Negro, by M. Anderson. *Annals of the American Academy*, January.

Relation of industrial education to national progress, by B. T. Washington. *Annals of the American Academy*, January.

Rural industrial school. *Nation*, April 22.

Self-help among the Negroes, by M. N. Work. *Survey*, August 7.

Church and the Negroes, by S. H. Bishop. *Spirit of Missions*, March.

Past and present among the Negroes of Southern Virginia, by J. S. Russell. *Spirit of Missions*, April.

Negroes of Pittsburg, by H. A. Tucker. *Charities*, January 2.

Banquo's ghost of American politics. *Current Literature*, July.

Cheerful journey through Mississippi, by B. T. Washington. *World's Work*, February.

Forced labor in America and the Alabama contract law. *Outlook*, December 19.

Georgia Negroes and their fifty millions of savings, by W. E. B. Du Bois, il. *World's Work*, May.

Georgia race strike. *Harper's Weekly*, June 12.

Georgia railroad strike. *Outlook*, June 5.

Georgia strike arbitration. *Harper's Weekly*, July 3.

Nearing a solution. *Outlook*, December 19.

Negro labor and the boll weevil, by A. H. Stone. *Annals of the American Academy*, March.

Negro problem in foreign eyes. *Nation*, Feb. 18.

New South. *Outlook*, July 17.

Notable Negro journey, by W. S. Dodd. *Independent*, April 22.

Pap Singleton, the Moses of the colored Exodus, by W. L. Fleming. *American Journal of Sociology*, July.

Patriarch's progeny, by H. Dickson. May.

President, the south and the Negro. by J. C. Hemphill. *Harper's Weekly*, January 9.

Report of friendly relations, by B. T. Washington. May 1.

South and the Negro, by S. G. Fisher. April 1.

Strange preference. *Independent*, April 8.

Studies in the American race problem, by A. H. Stone. *Yale Review*, August.

Race factor in education, by V. McCaughey. *Educational Review*, September.

Lincoln-Douglass debates and their application to present problems, by H. Taylor. February.

Negro's life in slavery, by B. T. Washington. *Outlook*, September 11.

Short course for farmers, by M. N. Work. *Outlook*, April 17.

Heart of a class problem. *Nation*, March 18.

The Unknowable Negro, by Harris Dickson. *Hampton's*, June.

26

The Over-Look

Ten thousand ears will hear the audacious lie,
One thousand to the refutation list,
Ten of ten thousand will believe stern truth.
W. W. Story.

THE NEW HORIZON

The enlarged edition of the HORIZON is an experiment in many ways. First, it is a frank acknowledgement of the fact that a Negro Magazine of a certain grade and appealing to a comparative small class, does not pay, in the sense that its income in the open market will not probably meet its expenses. With many persons this is conclusive argument that the periodical is not needed. But does this follow? By no means. Certain vehicles of thought, defense and exposition are often needed even when they are not commercially profitable—that is even when many of those for whom they work are not convinced of their need. Of course it is a question how far any one should attempt to cater to a people beyond their self-known needs; perhaps the chief distinction between business and philanthropy lies herein. But certainly whether we call it business or charity it is one of the highest duties of men that those who see a great need should do what they can to fulfill it even if the service does not pay in cash. Today the guarantors and supporters of the HORIZON think that they see a great need; they may be mistaken but judging from the past and from the developments among other people around about them, there is today among Negro Americans a great necessity of teaching certain broad truths both to the race itself and to the surrounding group of white Americans. The motives and method of this band of men and those of their way of thinking has been falsified and persistently misrepresented. We are called agitators in the sense of irresponsible persons who get their chief amusement and their daily bread by making a noise; yet we must remember that some of the greatest movements in the world's history have been led by men who were also called agitators, and who were agitators in the sense that they tried to arouse the conscience of a nation or of a group to certain persistent wrongs. We have been called pessimists, and we are pessimists, if by pessimist you mean a man who clearly sees a present evil. Of course the proper interpretation of the word pessimist is one who believes that all things are going wrong; but a pessimist in this sense is more apt to keep silent than to speak or to agitate; for why should he speak and agitate if all is going wrong? A man, however, who believes that the tendencies of the world are right but that there are great and

From *The Horizon: A Journal of the Color Line* 5 (January 1910): 1–4, 7.

trying wrongs, and who speaks against those wrongs because he believes that they can be righted is not a pessimist but an optimist. On the other hand any Negro American today who can be lightly and joyfully happy over his present situation is neither pessimist nor optimist, but simply a fool. What we need to do is to face the present situation manfully and to ask ourselves, What is going to right our present wrongs?

We, then, who stand behind the HORIZON, are those who especially believe that there are wrongs which the Negro is suffering; that those wrongs can be righted, and we believe above all that the methods of democracy are the methods by which those wrongs can best be righted. We believe that the Negro ought to be unfettered in speaking for himself; that he should have a chance for self-realization and self-expression in all legitimate lines; and that the endeavor to curb his liberty, to keep him from doing his own thinking and his own speaking is vicious—just as vicious in the case of Negro Americans as it was in the case of Americans of 1776.

The HORIZON, then is a demand for democracy—spiritual freedom for ten millions of people, and not for these only but for all men the world over. This is, we freely admit a large program, difficult to realize, but it is the ideal toward which we go. Of course our full plans of publication cannot be realized in these initial numbers; we plan more departments and a better grade of work in future.

In order now to carry out this plan we need in the first place, subscribers, and we want to urge all people whether they believe exactly as we do or whether they simply believe in freedom, to subscribe and to get others to subscribe.

ANNIVERSARIES

We are nearing the years of jubilee; we are coming to the days when with propriety we can look back upon the history of the arduous past and pause now and then in our daily life and recall by celebration, and reading and writing and worship various milestones in the history of the Negro race in America.

There are so many anniversaries at hand that it would be almost invidious to pick out certain ones, and yet the following we cannot forget: October 16th, of last year was the fiftieth anniversary of John Brown's raid, and December 2nd, the Jubilee of his martyrdom. Two years later in 1911, June 14th, comes the one hundredth anniversary of the birth of Harriet Beecher Stowe; the Jubilee of Emancipation comes January 1st, 1913; in that same year, July 18th, the fiftieth anniversary of the celebrated battle of Fort Wagner, and on July 13th, the fiftieth anniversary of Draft Riots in New York. In 1914 we may in March celebrate the three hundred and seventy-fifth anniversary of the discovery of the South-west by Estevanico, or, to translate his name, Stephen Dorantes. In 1915 comes the Jubilee of the Thirteenth Amendment; in 1917 the centennial of the birth of Frederick Douglass; in 1918 the fiftieth anniversary of the passage of the Fourteenth Amendment, and finally as a great climax, in 1919, August, the three hundreth anniversary of the landing of the black man in America.

HAYTI

I have, I confess, read with much sorrow the comment of many colored editors concerning the recent revolution in Hayti. Many have followed their white brethren by rushing into print and reading various sorts of severe lectures to this island of the Sea. Few of the men who have done this, however, have any very clear idea of the history of Hayti or of its present condition; to such men I only recommend a reading of Mr. Leger's book on Hayti. It can be obtained of the Neale Company in Washington for a small sum, and before any one else dares to say or write anything concerning this Negro Republic he should at least read a part of this book.

Let us as Negro Americans not forget the services which Hayti has done to the world. Above all events the revolution in Hayti proved to the Modern world the essential manhood of the black slave. Up to that time it has been said, with some truth, that it seemed possible to enslave the Negro where other races would have revolted. This assertion was not altogether true; men forgot the terrible Maroons of Jamaica and the various other revolts in other islands; but these had not filled the public eye enough to convince folk. The revolution under Toussaint L'Overture was, however, a vast and undeniable fact. Nor did Hayti stop here. When the United States was fighting for its freedom the black men from Hayti helped her in the celebrated siege of Savannah, and with unexampled bravery covered the retreat of the American troops; when South America was fighting for freedom Simon Bolivar went to Hayti and there obtained troops, money and supplies twice in succession, which enabled him to make South America free.

It may be that the black men of North America will yet find if not physical at least spiritual aid and encouragement from this little island in their own struggle. The revolution which has recently taken place was one which every one who knew the present condition of Hayti expected must come sooner or later.

Hayti stands between two great difficulties; she is economically undeveloped, yet if she allows foreign capital to come in and help her development foreign political control will only too soon follow. Her natural market is the United States, but the United States has for a century shut out her products by almost prohibitive tariff rates. In striving then through conservative action from falling into economic slavery to modern European organized trade, Hayti very easily falls into the opposite difficulty of ultra conservatism.

Nord Alexis was a man of the extreme conservative type, a leader like the old African chieftain, a man who not only guarded his country against the baneful influence of outsiders, but stood too against all sorts of new ideas and innovations. The progressive Haytians found themselves utterly choked and held in bay by this strong old man, and at last it was seen that only by physical revolution could they gain the chance to make that slow and careful progress which Hayti is continually making. The revolution was carried out with unusual quiet and care; there was little blood-shed, little upheaval; the picturesque old man was sent away, and a new and more progressive man put in his place.

Let us hope that the little island, which has so bravely kept its independence so far will still keep it in the future and that it can always count upon the sympathy and good-will of Negro Americans.

1909	1909
Credit	Debit
Matthew Henson reached the North Pole.	William Taft becomes President.
Disfranchisement is beaten a second time in Maryland.	Mr. Booker T. Washington is continued as political leader and distributor of Federal patronage.
The Lincoln Centennial culminates in a great Race Conference in New York	No Negro is appointed to office and seven

and a forward movement.

Mr. Kennedy and Miss Stokes leave money for Negro education.

White Georgia skilled labor strikes against the efficiency of Black skilled labor and is partially beaten.

A commission goes to Liberia.

John Brown is remembered.

New York honors the soldiers whom Roosevelt and Taft seek to disgrace.

One hundred books and articles on Negro Americans are published.

Three hundred Negro newspapers and periodicals are issued.

Jack Johnson whips all white men who dare fight him.

Property rapidly accumulates and business enterprise expands.

Negroes are replaced by whites.

The colored public school system of Washington is plunged into personal politics and torn with dissension.

Foraker after a splendid fight for us retires.

South Africa refuses the franchise to Negroes.

Black Berea is still disestablished.

General Howard dies.

Ninety-eight Negroes are lynched.

The Balance

We have progressed. The chains are still clanking, the coward and the traitor are still at large, the poor and guilty and unfortunate are still with us. Our enemies smile. So do we. We have progressed.

LITERATURE

Some mistakes in the review of literature last month were inevitable. Perhaps the greatest was in forgetting to mention the name of William Stanley Braithwaite, the undoubted poet-laureate of our race in America. His small but exquisite work has continued to appear in the *Atlantic* and elsewhere during the last year.

Notwithstanding all that writers have done, however, the number of us who think and write is disappointingly small. Nor is the reason far to seek; why aspire and delve for Art's sake and Truth's when you can make MONEY? What is literature compared with bricks? This devilish materialistic philosophy which is rife among us is killing ambition, destroying merit and manufacturing thieves, liars and flunkeys. How long, O Lord, how long shall we bow tongue-tied or double-tongued before our enemies?

BOOKS

There is something pathetic about Mr. Murphy's book. Here is a Southerner making a brave fight against Death; against physical death, for he has long been a sick man; against spiritual death, for he wants to be both a Southerner and a Christian. His book says, with careful, almost painful elaboration, and in slow and cautious movement: Let the Negro develop, break the chains, throw down the barriers, because after all he is but little more than a half-man and cannot possibly develop far enough to threaten your God-given supremacy. This is the main thesis of the *Basis of Ascendency* through eleven chapters and 248 pages. One rises from the book with the same feeling that one rose from its predecessor, *The Present South*. Jane Addams once voiced that feeling: she said the book was "too good not to be just a little better."

27

The Over-Look

"Ole Uncle S., sez he, 'I guess
" 'It is fact,' sez he,
" 'The surest plan to make a man
" 'Is, think him so, J. B.,
" 'Ez much ez you or me.' "

Lowell.

PERIODICALS

African Game Trails, IV. Theodore Roosevelt. Scribner. Jan.
The Vanishing Indians. C. W. Furlong. Harper. Jan.
African Game Trails, V. Theodore Roosevelt. Scribner. Feb.
Barbarbous, Mexico. Herman Whitaker. American. Feb.
Prohibition in Alabama. Robert Hiden. World To-day. Feb.
Reconstruction Period, Diary of. Gideon Welles. Atlantic. Feb.

An interesting pamphlet which comes to us is written by Geo. W. Carver and describes some of the ornamental plants of Macon County, Alabama. It is illustrated and well printed.

J'ACCUSE

I accuse the white South of five unexcusable present wrongs:
1. Of seeking class Subordination under the name of "Race Separation."
2. Of seeking the Seduction of black women under the name of "Racial Integrity."
3. Of seeking Industrial Slavery under the name of "Negro Disfranchisement."
4. Of seeking the perpetuation of Ignorance under the name of "Industrial Education."
5. Of seeking Oligarchy under the name of "White Supremacy."
6. Of upholding Paganism in place of "Christianity."

I have no word to say to the man who does not wish my company.

I have no dispute with the woman who declines to marry me.

I have no defence of the voter who is wilfully ignorant of his duties and responsibilities.

From *The Horizon: A Journal of the Color Line* 5 (February 1910): 1–4.

I believe in industrial education.
I believe in the defence of civilization.
And I believe in the moral code of Jesus Christ.

———

But I refuse to be called lacking in self-respect when I oppose "Jim Crow" legislation.

I refuse to be called ashamed of my race when I call the marriage laws of the South barbarous, and the sexual practices worse than barbarous.

I refuse to be dubbed an impatient politician when I assert that the Negro's right to vote is fundamental to his right to work.

I refuse to be called "impractical" and "visionary" when I see the Negro public schools ruined, and the colleges cheapened by miserable deceptions set to tickle the ears and the pocket books of gullible philanthropists.

I refuse to be called uncharitable when I say that the white South has absolutely nothing in common with Jesus Christ.

You cannot physically "separate" people today without turning back civilization one thousand years. Even at that time separation had to be absolute and complete or it meant conquest, slavery and caste. It means the same today and only fools are unaware of the fact.

For the white South to stand up straight-faced in the eyes of millions of mulattoes and prate of "racial integrity" is a piece of damnable hyprocrisy that shrieks to heaven. The cure is clear: Make the white man marry and support his black paramour and support his children, instead of shaming only the woman and stigmatizing the child.

Wage slavery has succeeded chattel slavery. It is saved from similar depths of horror by the laborer's vote and the fear that some day he may awake to use it. Deprive him of that vote and he's helpless. Do you think that the exploiters of the South do not know this?

In educating a child one of the prime and indispensable things is to give him the key to further knowledge by teaching him to read, write and cipher. Without this, and with how much so ever else he may learn he is shut to eternal darkness and ignorance of modern life. Yet today our children are being taught to cook and whittle before they can read, and thousands never learn to read decently because they are busy learning "scientific agriculture." To Hell with such lying deception of the young and helpless.

It is true that the lighter skinned races are leading civilization today. It is not true that civilization is the invention of the white race or that they have made the greatest contributions to it. It is false that any race has or ever will have a right to monopolize the earth and its fruit, or the human mind and its thoughts. "White Supremacy" is the last scared yell of the dog about to be beaten.

Is the South Christian? Read the Sermon on the Mount.

1909

One decided credit to 1909 which I inadvertently omitted last month was Deneen's dismissal of the sheriff who permitted the lynching at Cairo, Ill. A committee of fourteen Chicago Negroes waited on Governor Deneen and strengthened

his back bone and he wrote, as Ida B. Wells Barnett, priestess of the Antilynching
Crusade reminds me:

> "Mob violence has no place in Illinois. It is denounced in every line of the
> Constitution and in every statute. Instead of breeding respect for the law, it
> breeds contempt. For the suppression of mob violence, our legislature has spoken
> in no uncertain terms. When such mob violence threatens the life of a prisoner
> in the custody of the sheriff, the law has charged the sheriff, at the penalty of
> a forfeiture of his office, to use the utmost human endeavor to protect the life
> of his prisoner. The law may be severe. Whether severe or not, it must be
> enforced.
> "Believing as I do that Frank E. Davis, as Sheriff of Alexander County, did
> not do all within his power to protect the lives of William James and Henry
> Salzner, I must deny the petition of said Frank E. Davis, for reinstatement as
> Sheriff of Alexander County, and the same is done accordingly."

JOHN F. COOK

We hear today wide-spread demand for Negro business men coupled with talk
that makes it seem that the black business man must be a truckler, a compromiser,
a traitor and a coward. John F. Cook was a living witness to the falsity of this
assumption. He was a successful business man, yet he bore himself in dignity,
demanded recognition as a man received it, and was never afraid to speak out for
the rights of his people. As a member of the Niagara Movement he showed even
in later years that he dared stand and be counted among men willing to suffer for
the right.

His death in the fulness of years and honors and in the bosom of a worthy
family is Death at its highest and best.

THE BAHAMAS

There lies before me No. 615 of the Colonial Reports of the British Empire.
It is the annual report of the governor of the Bahama Islands for 1908–09, and
there is in it much food for thought when we compare conditions in the Bahamas
with those in the United States. The Bahamas had, it is estimated, 60,309 inhabitants
in 1908, practically all of whom are colored except a small handful of officials. We
may, therefore, compare this colored population with the Negroes of the United
States. They have a birth rate of 34 and a death rate of 26 per thousand. No one
knows the birth rate in the United States because no statistics are kept. The death
rate is below that of the Negroes in the United States, so far as we know that rate
for any considerable member. To be sure there is a reported death rate of 19 1/
16 for rural districts of a few registration states but this comprehends only a few
Negroes. For the most part in the registration districts the death rate is 30 2/10
thousand.

The population in the Bahamas is taken care of by 104 policemen and the
arrests in 1908 amounted to 42½ per thousand of population. In the city of Savannah
the arrests at the same time were 150 per thousand and in Atlanta they ranged
from 265 to 223 per thousand. This of course does not mean that the Negroes in
the United States are from three to eight times as criminal as those of the Bahamas
but it does mean that here we have a wretched judicial and police system and that
the Negroes are the victims of it.

This is proven further by the fact that while we see in the Northern cities, where the judicial system is better, from 1 5/10 to 4 4/10 per thousand of the Negro population were committed to the penitentiary, in Nassau, on the other hand, this proportion sinks to less than one per thousand, or 55 out of a population of over sixty thousand.

Turning to education we find in Nassau sixty government schools and schools receiving government aid and fifty private schools with with 9,540 pupils in all on the average roll. There must be in Nassau a considerable number of children not in school but, nevertheless, there is a compulsory law, the upper limit of which has been raised from 13 to 14 years. No Southern community of the United States has, as yet, any such law. The government schools are fairly well provided with teachers, there being one to each 33 pupils in attendance. This is a much better condition than in the Negro schools of the South. The average cost per child in average attendance is about six dollars per year. In the United States it is officially reported for Negro children between $2.25 and $2.60 and actually it is not much over $1.50.

The chief defect in the Nassau schools would seem to be no state provision for secondary education. There are four private secondary schools but they have only 150 pupils. The most of these are schools primarily for white officials' children. No state can expect to raise up the thinking and leading class of people, such as the West Indies needs, without better provision for higher education than this. The chief income of Nassau is from customs duties and licenses. The chief expenditures are for debt, post office and salaries. The latter apparently taking the larger part of the income. On the whole what is being done for the colored people of Nassau is evidently being far better done than we are accomplishing in the United States, but there would seem to be a distinct room for diverting some of the money paid in salaries to English officials toward education and social reform.

SLANDER

There is running in a current magazine of the lower sensational type a series of articles on "Miscegenation." They are a shameless attempt to shoulder on the Negro the responsibility of the White Man's peculiar plague: Venereal diseases. They would hardly be worth noticing was not one of the articles bolstered up by a letter from C. W. Stiles of Hookworm fame, virtually assenting to the monstrous thesis of these articles. I have written the Department of the Treasury under which Stiles works asking if a public official is to be allowed thus to slander ten million American citizens. I hope you will do the same. We may not stop the slander's mouth in this instance but we may prepare a well deserved gag for the future.

BLACK WOMEN

Miss Ida Tarbell, in the American Magazine has at last discovered Africa in her history of American women. To be sure it is only a caricature of the noble Sojourner Truth and the words put in her mouth are a hideous and ridiculous dialect such as no human being ever spoke. Still it is interesting to have Miss Tarbell recognize at last that there are black folk in America. The fact has escaped her hitherto.

28

The Over-Look

Wherever brother hands are clasped and tight
Resolved to battle for the trampled Right.
There is thy sacrament for which I search—
There is my altar, there my holy church.

—Edwin Markham

BETTER SOUTH

It has been suggested that when I "accuse the White South," I arraign not simply those guilty of the faults alleged but many persons who oppose such deeds. This is true if by "White South" one understands all white Southerners. In my mind "White South" stood for the efficient, dominant, acting South. Of this South my strictures are true.

There is always among men, however, a saving remnant. There is in the white South of today such a body of men. They may be classified as follows:

1. Those who openly and persistently oppose the South's
Negro program.
2. Those who oppose the Negro program but who speak
out and act only occasionally.
3. Those who do not believe in the radical program and
vote against its specific proposals from time to time, but in
the end submit quietly to the majority, and even defend it.

The first class is small enough almost to be named personally: Cable, Walter Page, Sledd, Ewing, and the like. It is significant that most of these earnest men have found the intellectual climate of the North most agreeable.

The second class is larger and tends to absorb those of the first who give up in despair. Many a southerner has taken one brave stand for the Negro and then thrown up his hands in despair—the social and economic forces are too strong. He becomes a silent man—his heart is right, he says, but he cannot afford speech or action.

The third class is large. It includes the large minorities who have opposed disfranchisement and segregation laws. It is not, however, a class of deep moral convictions and its actions have been largely dictated by expediency. Nevertheless, it has voted, spoken and acted right on occasions. The chief trouble with this class is that it lacks abiding principles. It has not made up its mind. It seeks with the

---

From *The Horizon: A Journal of the Color Line* 5 (March 1910): 1–5.

same breath to bind Negroes in a hopeless place of inferiority and then treat them "fairly." It tries to acknowledge with one breath that the Negro should be allowed to rise and then without a trial denies him most of the chances for advancement, especially the chance of self-respect. Yet withal this class is far better than the worst.

To all these classes I give thanks and appreciation. They are, for the most part, honest, striving men. Some have seen the light; some are earnestly seeking it. I praise them. I help them. I cooperate with them when I may. But they are not "The White South" and they know it.

THE NEGRO AND THE Y.M.C.A.

On February 20th I spoke at the Central "White" Young Men's Christian Association, 23rd Street, New York, at their repeated invitation.

There are in the United States 39 city and 91 student associations composed of colored men, with 17,000 members. Through the devoted work of Hunton, Moorland, Haynes and Watson this work has grown and expanded. Notwithstanding this the white associations are drawing the color line even in the North. Therefore, I spoke to these young white men as follows:

A Man's Right

"A man today, be he black or white, Jew or Gentile, rich or poor, has a right to ask in the hands of the public a certain fairness of treatment as preliminary to his own efforts. Now, the thing he asks for or the fair show which he demands is, in the thought of the most careless persons, something that they must give from their abundance. You think of the figure of the race-track: to give each runner a fair show you must stand aside and perhaps be yourself crowded; or you think of your passing through the streets: to give your fellow passenger a fair show you must keep to the right and walk slowly and watch the vehicles.

"Now in that chance which men ask for in the world, there is involved, to be sure, something of this personal carefulness and sacrifice; but it does not, as many seem to suppose, stop here; on the contrary here is where it begins. The real thing is not the giving up of something that belongs to you but the refraining to appropriate wholly to yourself that which belongs to him just as well as to you. And, therefore, instead of saying: 'Give us a fair show,' the world of tomorrow is going to turn to you and say: 'Do not take unfair advantage,' for this is the other side of the same ethical problem.

"Now to understand just what is meant here let us consider certain elementary things: A man is living on a great Southern plantation or a lonesome Western ranch. He may be rich and talented and physically strong and yet there are many things which he misses and must forego: streets to walk upon, streetcars ready at his command in every and any direction, theaters to entertain him, restaurants with meals always prepared, lecturers ready to talk, policemen ready to defend, parks, museums, gardens; all these things he cannot have, either not at all, or in an extremely limited form. When now, that same man comes to live in a town or city, more so in a great city, there are numbers of these things which he can have at his command, either for nothing or for slight expense, and the reason that he has them is not because they belong to him, in the sense of ownership, or because he is a person of unusual desert, but primarily and essentially because other people are living with him and wanting the same things, and the presence of masses of men with their assembled desires, wealth and power make possible for them things which of themselves as individuals they could not dream of commanding. Thus it is that the individual becomes a member of the state; a partner in the group.

The Temptation

"But no sooner does he become such partner than his first besetting temptation is to forget whence these benefits come.

"Mankind forgot so completely in the earlier years of human civilization that the state was looked upon, not as the contribution of *all* to *each* and of *each* to *all,* but rather as a peculiar property of the few, even of one: 'I am the state,' said the typical monarch of the 17th century, and 'We are Society,' has been the cry of small and exclusive aristocracies then and since. Of course, as matter of fact, there is not a single individual that by any stretch of imagination can arrogate to himself ownership of that which by right of creation belongs to all. New York is possible not simply because of the dwellers on Fifth Avenue but also because of the dwellers on the lower East Side, and each would be unthinkable, impossible, without the other. Now, we are beginning to learn this lesson, but we have not learned it thoroughly.

"Almost any intelligent man today would admit that the state without organized society cannot be thought of as the property of any privileged few individuals, but there are still large numbers of us who are willing and somewhat eager to think there are certain parts of us, and certain human beings, whom it is right and a sort of duty to shut out from the advantages of organization. We are willing, and rather glibly, to say that the state is for all but in that *all* we do not count everybody. We exclude, as the chance may lie, Chinese, or Jews, or Negroes or women. I come to impress upon you the fact that no such exclusion can be made without injustice or harm.

"An individual has a perfect right to his private preferences; to singling out his own companions, to going with his own clique, but when he steps out of his private domain and takes advantage of the public bounty then he has no right to use that public bounty as if it were his private fortune. He has the right, for instance, to go to the theatre and take his own friends, but he has no right to stop me from going to the theatre and taking my friends; for the theatre is a public institution made possible by the coming together of great aggregations of men; made possible by public education paid for by the taxes of all; made possible by the whole social organization, of which it is to some extent an expression.

The Y. M. C. A.

"Now, what is true in this respect is true in an organization like the Young Men's Christian Association. I confess that I have come to address this Central Young Men's Christian Association in New York with no feeling of pleasure, and this, not because I am not in sympathy with your work, for I am. I remember, in my boyhood years ago, the meetings of the struggling Christian Association in a New England town; the singing, the sprightly addresses were to me a source of pleasure—an inspiration. I find too, theoretically, in all of your greater objects an unusual sympathy. This is an organization of young men, with all that youth and manhood means. Youth with its possibility of learning and inspiring and uplifting, and manhood with its ideals of strength and fairness.

"Then, too, it is not only an association of young men but it is an association which professes to follow the system of ethics laid down by Jesus Christ, and that system of ethics states in broader and stronger language than I have, not simply the right of each individual, no matter how humble, to a place in the state and in public organization, but also, further than that, insists with reiterated emphasis upon the duty of every individual to make his neighbor's enjoyment of the public bounty of just as much importance as his own. 'Thou shalt love thy neighbor as thyself,' Now with all this theoretical predilection for the Young Men's Christian Association, why is it that I enter, not particularly this association, but indeed most associations of this kind of the country with a distinct feeling of distaste and antagonism? It is of course, as you know, chiefly because if I or my brother or my child wished to become a member of this association, to enjoy the bounty and advantages which you are enjoying, and which are very largely a free gift to you. I would be excluded, either peremptorily or by evasive and underhanded means or by unbearable treatment; and I come to you to say frankly that such action on the part of an organization like this, *is neither an exhibition of manhood nor in accordance with the right ideals of youth nor in accordance with the ethics of Jesus Christ*, or, in other words, it isn't fair.

Manhood, and the Ideals of Youth

"I say in the first place it is not *manly* because you are taking and holding for yourselves, and refusing to share with others that which does not belong to you. The Young Men's Christian Associations throughout the land and throughout the world are the gifts of good men and efforts of philanthropists and the results of the social groupings in which they are located. They are the property of no race or clique; they belong to the community which they seek to serve, and yet there is a tendency toward monopolizing them. This tendency is shown in its grossest and most indefensible form in race discrimination against Negroes; but it is also shown in other forms both as to race and as to class, and in whatever form it is shown it is an exhibition of an unmanly spirit; it is taking for yourself that which belongs to others; not being satisfied with enjoying the bounty of society yourself, but being determined that your neighbor shall not enjoy it.

"Further than that, as I have said, such racial exclusiveness and class spirit is not in accordance with the *ideals of youth*. Youth is the hope of tomorrow. It is the unfinished and growing power that is going to build a better world and better men to people the world. Whoever, then, poisons the ideals of youth poisons the spring out which we are going to expect the greater purity and honesty and justice of that world to flow. The ideals of youth then are ideals of progress, and from the time of the ancient exclusive clan down until the 20th century the history of progress has been the history of the death of personal and racial prejudice, and the widening of the spirit of humanity.

"There was a time when the duty of a man was laid down as being the loving of his kinspeople and hate and death to everybody else. When by growth his kinspeople became his nation, then his duty was to love his country and hate all other countries; and now that the intercourse of the world has brought men to such knowledge that they recognize few bounds of countries and governments, there are still those who strive to say: 'You shall love and promote the advantages of those of your own race, and despise and exclude those of all other races.' More and more today this exclusion tends to segregation along the color line. It is not so much a matter of personal feeling as it is a half-hidden desire to do the proper thing. Men newly come to America, and Americans come to great centers of civilization like New York, quickly discover that among men and their neighbors it is deemed smart and proper to despise black folk, and without further to do, or further extending of any personal knowledge, and with indeed but little thought, you are apt to adopt such prejudices as your own, and to put discredit and evil not only upon ten million of your own fellow citizens but upon hundreds of millions the world over.

The Religion of Jesus Christ

"Further than this, as I have said, such racial exclusion is not in accordance with the *Religion of Jesus Christ*. Jesus Christ was a man who despised the prejudices of his time; who associated with and loved people to whom his fellow countrymen would disdain even to speak: who discovered among the lowest and meekest the loftiest and sweetest souls and who laid it down as a guiding rule of life to 'Do unto others even as you would that others would do unto you.'

"Now, as I have said, here is an organization which gathers up unto itself the ideals of youth, the honorable conduct of manhood and the ethics of Jesus Christ, and yet proceeds to break these ideals; to discredit the honor and refuses to follow the ethical teachings of its master.

"But I know that we today are not moved as much as we should be by ethical discourses on duty and honor. We pride ourselves in being something which we call practical. We say: 'It may be as matter of fact a beautiful theory all right to judge men of black skins by exactly the same criterion as we judge other men, but the thing is not practical, and it is not practical because these two races are so different that the same rules of honor and hope and righteousness do not apply to both.' This answer of the man that is doing persistently wrong is not new.

"The nobles of the old regime, in France, despised the dog of a peasant because, as they said, he was not a man in the same sense as they were. The Russian of today despises the Jew because, as he says, the Jew is not entitled to be treated as the same sort of human being as the Russian. The English capitalist of the 18th Century despised the workingman because, as he said, they were an entirely different order of folk than he and his. And so today, the American having struggled up out of that hell of prejudice and discredit and wrong, still yields to that desire of despising somebody and says, 'The Negro does not belong to the same grade of humanity as we.'

"And yet what is the fact? The fact is that the very thing that France needed was that the noble and peasant should really know each other, and when they really did know each other, they respected each other. They were different: different by training and heredity, but difference does not necessarily mean inferiority: it may mean incompleteness.

"So, too, the thing that is doing more than any other thing to settle modern labor troubles is the fact that the boss and laborer are coming to know each other as men; not as the same men– they are not the same—they are different by training and even by heredity, but each man is learning something from the other, and when they have learned it, the settlement of labor disputes is in sight.

"So, too, with the Negro problem in the United States. The Negro and the white man are different; different by training and heredity, but as I have said, differences themselves do not necessarily mean inferiority or superiority; they may mean incompleteness. And there is nothing that the modern white world needs more than certain things which characterize the Negro; just as it is also true that the Negro has much to learn of the white world. But above all, the thing which men, black and white, rich and poor, high and low, must learn is that the day for despising human beings is long passed, and that given a man of any color or of any race, who deserves to be treated as a man, it is not simply un-Christian but anti-social and in the end fatal, to treat him otherwise than as his desert demands; and to this eternal fact I call the attention of the Young Men's Christian Association today."

The Good of It

There was prolonged applause; and yet
What good does it do to talk like this?
"It's foolish," say some; "It's vain," say others; "It's false," say a few. But I answer but one thing, "It is True!" and—the Truth shall make us free!

———

There are great truths that pitch their shining tents
    Outside our walls, and though but dimly seen
In the gray dawn, they will be manifest
    When the light widens into perfect day.

H. W. Longfellow.

29

The Over-Look

"At the outer edge of the world
Where the long grey mists arise
Between the sunset and the sea
I gaze with longing eyes."
—Braithwaite.

SUBSCRIBERS

If the HORIZON is to live, it must have one thousand more subscribers by September first. No one connected with the HORIZON makes anything out of it. The three editors have not only given their services free, but have, in the last three years, paid out $300 from their pockets to keep it going. If the people want it, we will proceed. If they do not, we cannot go on. You know one, two or five people who ought to take this paper. Speak to them and send us their names. Make a strenuous effort to have in the United States an unmuzzled monthly. Let us have at least 500 additional subscribers for the next issue. These are parlous times, friends; if you are not interested in yourselves, who will be interested?

THE UNIVERSAL RACES CONGRESS

A Congress, which promises to be one of the most influential of our time, is to be held in London in July, 1911. The list of those who have extended to it their moral support is perhaps the most imposing one of its kind. Among the supporters, who hail from no less than forty countries, are over twenty Presidents of Parliaments, about a hundred Members of the Permanent Court of Arbitration and of the Second Hague Conference, many present and past Statesmen and Ambassadors, some hundred and thirty Professors of International Law, the leading Anthropologists and Sociologists, the President, Treasurer, General Secretary and the majority of the Council of the Inter-Parliamentary Union, and other distinguished personages.

The Object of the Congress will be to discuss the larger racial issues in the light of modern knowledge and the modern conscience, with a view to encouraging a good understanding, friendly feelings, and hearty co-operation between Occidental and Oriental peoples. Political issues of the hour will be subordinated to this comprehensive end, in the firm belief that when once mutual respect is established,

From *The Horizon: A Journal of the Color Line* 5 (May 1910): 1–4

difficulties of every type will be sympathetically approached and readily solved.

The origin of this Congress is readily explained. The interchange of material and spiritual goods between the different races of mankind has of late years assumed such dimensions that the old attitude of distrust and aloofness is giving way to a general desire for closer acquaintanceship. Out of this interesting situation has sprung the idea of holding a Congress where the representatives of the different races might meet each other face to face, and might, in friendly rivalry, further the cause of so-called white peoples and the so-called coloured peoples.

Accordingly the Congress will not represent a meeting of all the races for the purpose of discussing indiscriminately everybody's concerns. It will not discuss purely European questions, such as the relations existing between or within the different European countries: nor, of course, will it discuss the attitude of Europe towards the United States or towards other American republics representing faces of European descent. Again, whilst wholly sympathetic towards all far-sighted measures calculated to strengthen and promote good relations, the Congress is pledged to no political party and to no particular scheme of reforms. The writers of papers will, however, have the full right to express whatever political views they may hold, though they will be expected to do justice to all political parties and to treat the issues of the day only passingly. Furthermore, the Congress will not be purely scientific in the sense of only stating facts and not passing judgments. Nor will it be a peace congress in the sense of aiming specifically at the prevention of war. Finally, it should be noted that, since the Congress is to serve the purpose of bringing about healthier relations between Occident and Orient, all bitterness towards parties, peoples, or governments will be avoided, without, of course, excluding reasoned praise and blame. With the problem simplified in this manner and with a limited number of papers by leading authorities who will elucidate the object of the Congress, there is every hope that the discussions will bear a rich harvest of good, and contribute materially towards encouraging friendly feelings and hearty co-operation between the peoples of the West and the East.

The following is the Programme for the nine half-day Sessions: 1. Fundamental Considerations—Meaning of Race and Nation. 2-3. Conditions for National Self-Government and Common Tendencies towards Parliamentary Rule. 4. Peaceful contact between civilisations. 5. Special Problems in Inter-Racial Economics. 6-7. The Modern Conscience in Relation to Racial Questions. 8-9. Positive Suggestions for Promoting Inter-Racial Friendliness. (To assist adequate discussion the papers are to be sent to Members of the Congress a month before the gathering, and will be taken as read; abstracts of the papers, in the four Congress languages, will also be provided.)

It is proposed also to hold in connection with the Congress an exhibition of books, documents, portraits, diagrams, etc.

Attendance at the meetings of the Congress will not be restricted to any particular class of persons. Fee for Active Membership (including attendance, volume of papers, and other publications) will be 21s., for Passive Membership (excluding attendance, but including volume of papers and other publications) 7s. 6d.

Further information may be obtained from the Hon. Organiser, Mr. G. Spiller, 63 South Hill Park, Hampstead, London: or from the American co-Secretaries, Prof. W. E. B. DuBois, Atlanta University, and Mr. Alfred W. Martin, 995 Madison Avenue, New York—*Circular*.

MY LETTER BOX

My letters are always interesting but at times they seem addressed not simply to me but to those who think with me. Therefore, this month I publish a few:

———

Madison, Wis., March 29, 1910.

MY DEAR MR. DUBOIS:

I have just read your resolute communication to the Boston Transcript: I had also read the garbled report that necessitated your reply. As a Negro-American I want to thank you for the brave fight that you are making for the race: and bid you continue in your intrepid way. The odds against you are tremendous; numbers, money, prejudice, selfishness and what not: but for all that you and your few fellows are leavening the whole loaf.

Race prejudice in this country stands ready to make prosperous and a BOSS of any Negro who will be the pliant tool in the effort to flatten-out the Negro to fit in the white man's prejudice. On the other hand, it seeks any means no matter how nefarious to consign to eternal damnation him who dares call a halt on their wicked designs.

The part that Mr. Booker T. Washington is playing with the well being of the entire Negro population of this country at stake, is abominable and thoroughly vicious. Industrial education which should be one of the mainstays in Negro uplift, is made by this truckling man an avenue through which the Negro is to be led to serfdom and kept there.†

———

Cholinogori, MARCH 16, 1910.

REVERED PROFESSOR:

We have read in one of our Russian magazines Mr. Rubinoff's very interesting article about his visit to the Atlanta University. All that he relates there surprises us very much. Is it possible that the American, who is so proud of his civilization and culture, could treat in such an inhuman manner his fellow-citizen only for the dark colour of his skin?

There is also in Russia a great deal of chauvinists of the worst sort, whom we call "the black sotnia." But they belong to that class of the Russian society who live by the help of the reigning darkness and oppression. But Mr. Rubinoff speaks about intelligent Americans, who are in the same time decided negrophobes and don't acknowledge human rights for the Negroes.

Such a thing we Russians cannot even understand. We are ourselves oppressed by the external might: we suffer very much in our struggle for liberty and progress. But it is only an external oppression and the society in its greater and best part professes the ideal of humane love for all nationalities, without difference between the Hellen and the Jew. So think we, the barbarous Russians, but the civilized Americans think otherwise.

We regret very much that we know nearly nothing about the condition of the coloured race in America: and if we know anything, it is from old, and sometimes not trustworthy sources. Excluding the excellent book of Beecher Stowe, we have very little, and even nothing in our language about the Negro questions.

We suffer ourselves very much, struggling for the new and free Russia, and sympathizing with our black brothers. We ardently wish to know about their condition. We don't want to hear neither the negrophobs, nor the negrophils, but those who think about your race as about *men*. Therefore we beg you, Revered Professor, if you will only have time, to write us what must we read to receive a true notion about the Negro question in North America. We could also translate this book into Russian, and hope that our countrymen will read it with great pleasure.

Finishing our letter we send our hearty greetings to the young Atlanta University and its students, and hope that the work of this Institution will lead to the regeneration and splendid future of the African race.

The representatives of the colony of political transports:

> N. COONIN.
> M. TAPDAGIUS.
> G. CHAULISKA.

Address: Cholmogori, Government Archangel, for student N. A. Coonin, Russia.

MY DEAR SIR: *Hoboken, N. J.,* MARCH 31, 1910.

I received a letter from you some time ago, and would have answered sooner, but I have been sick. You asked in your letter for the facts concerning my achievements. I graduated from Public School No. 9. Hoboken, N. J. with the following percentages: History 100, Geography 96, Grammar 100, Arithmetic 100, Civics 100, Spelling 100, with a general average of 99 1-3.

You spoke of me going through college, but as circumstances will not permit, I have decided to continue with my music and give lessons.

Sincerely yours.

> STELLA E. GIBBS.

DEAR SIR: *Jersey City, N. J.,* March 21, 1910

Your kind letter was received but owing to the continued illness of my mother and my school work, I have had no opportunity to answer it.

By "facts" I suppose you refer to the individual averages during the course. They are as follows:

MATHEMATICS

Elementary Algebra	93.33
Advanced Algebra	96
Plane Geometry	93.5
Solid Geometry	94
Plane Trigonomety	94

SCIENCE

Zoology	94
Physiology	90
Physics	94
Chemistry	93.5

HISTORY

Greek History 99
Roman History 96

LANGUAGES

German 90
English 93.87
Latin 95.43
Deportment 97

My averages in English and Latin were the highest in the class.

Thanking you for the interest you have taken in me and hoping that this is the desired information, I remain.

Yours respectfully,

THOMAS O. JOHNSON.

THE CATHOLIC CHURCH AND THE NEGRO

There are signs that the Catholic Church is awakening to its duty toward the Negro American. For years, Slattery of Baltimore struggled alone and in vain for adequate recognition for this race but the forces of prejudice were too strong for him and he was hushed.

The truth rose again and today the propaganda is going forward.

A writer in the St. Paul *Pioneer Press* says:

> The custom in the Catholic church of offering prayers on Good Friday for all classes of persons even "the perfidious Jews," since on that day "Christ died for all," had a dramatic setting in St. Paul's Cathedral yesterday which, were its meaning fully understood and heeded, would effectually solve the race problem in this country.
>
> Acting as deacon of the mass, standing at the right hand of the archbishop, second only to his grace in dignity, was a full-blooded negro. Frequently his duties made him the center of attention throughout the solemn and impressive ceremonies; especially when in a rich, musical voice, characteristic of his race, he sang the Gospel of Good Friday; again when he presented the image of the crucified Redeemer to the archbishop for the "veneration of the cross," and when, walking with him under the canopy carried by four white ecclesiastics, he assisted his grace to carry the consecrated host. Surely the doctrine that "all men are created equal" is fully realized in the Catholic church, which is no respecter of persons, even if it is not always and everywhere recognized in these United States.

This young priest was the Rev. Stephen L. Theobald who led his classes in the Seminary and will, it is hoped, be put at the head of the Colored Catholic Church in St. Paul—a church, by the way, which is not a "Jim Crow" institution, but has as many white as colored members.

Again in St. Louis a Catholic paper defends black men as follows:

> Priests build costly churches and incur heavy debts and they behold with consternation the departure of their best people, driven to more desirable quarters by the presence of the black families in their block. But what can be done? These negroes have as much right to own property and live in exclusive neighborhoods as white people. Must they be made to suffer for the race prejudice of their white neighbors? Priests must remember that the Church does not draw the color line, and will not permit it to be drawn by Catholics.

The Rev. John E. Burke of New York recently said:

> The colored people are what slavery made them. It robbed them of the power of self-direction and took from them the great civilizing power of the family life.
>
> The real colored problem consists in introducing the principles of justice and charity, the teachings of our Blessed Lord among the unschooled and some-what bigoted portion of the white population.

Watch the Catholic Church, my brothers, we may yet find there the Christianity which we miss in many Protestant denominations.

"ENDYMION'S DREAM"

Mr. Coleridge-Taylor has produced a new cantata which the London *Standard* describes as "a very striking novelty."

> Indeed, it contains some of the best music which the composer has given us since "Hiawatha." Virtually, it consists of a short prelude, an opening chorus, a couple of solos, and an extended love duet, punctuated by a running choral commentary, originally written for the stage with a hidden chorus. Seldom has so much urgent music—music that breathes and reeks of romance and passion in almost every bar—been compressed into so small a compass. At a time when the future of English opera is upon everyone's lips it is encouraging to meet with a work that reveals a sense of the theatre so unmistakably as does Mr. Coleridge-Taylor's so-called cantata.

The Daily *Telegram* says:

> But not since, in his student days, Mr. Coleridge-Taylor evolved the opening part of his "Hiawatha" trilogy, has he composed music that seemed so grateful and so inevitable.

Other papers add:

> The work will undoubtedly add to Mr. Coleridge-Taylor's laurels.—*Pall Mall Gazette.*

> The music shows that Mr. Coleridge-Taylor has a very remarkable sense of climax, and he has learnt how to make them strong metaphorically as well as physically—that is to say, intense as well as loud.—*The Star.*

> The new cantata will not improbably rank high among the composer's works, for it seems to mark a distinct advance in his musical individuality.—*Manchester Guardian.*

> From soft, luscious strains of awakening sentiment the emotion swells into ecstasy that becomes almost delirium, in the very climax of which the dream returns to visionless slumber. The composer has made the music croon with sentiment of sweetest, most delicious murmuring; he has made it pulsate with rich, warm jets of emotion in his strongest, most picturesque mood. Over it all, surely, is cast the very glamour of the pale moonlight.—*Brighton Gazette.*

Well done, our brother.

————

Why should men be valued according to accident of generation? This condition is certainly a lapse to barbarism deeper than any imagine. Men should not be condemned racially, but individually.

The world shall learn that it is not the race but the spirit; not the constitution of blood or color of skin, but conduct that differentiates between men.—Rabbi Hirsch.

EDITOR'S NOTE
†Elucidation of this letter, and the text of Du Bois's remarks in February 1910, concerning Booker T. Washington, are as follows:

On page ten of the May, 1910 issue of *The Horizon*, in the section called "The Outlook" edited by L.M. Hershaw, one finds the following quoted by the N.Y. *Evening Post* from Du Bois's letter in the Boston *Transcript:*

> Mr. Washington has for the last eight years allowed himself to be made the sole referee for all political action concerning 10,000,000 Americans. Few appointments of Negroes to office have been made without his consent, and others' political policies have been deferred to him. Now, if Mr. Washington was consulted solely because of his knowledge of men and wide acquaintanceship, there would be less ground of criticism. But, whatever the purpose, it has been inevitable that only those Negroes should be put in political control of black men who agree with Mr. Washington's policy of non-resistance, giving up of agitation, and acquiescence in semi-serfdom.

In the section of this same issue entitled "In-Look" (pages 10-11) edited by F.H.M. Murray a portion of an address by Du Bois delivered in Boston in February, 1910, is reprinted:

> We are coming to a time in the case of southern problems when the idealists ought to speak a solemn word of warning, and the nation ought to remember the legacy of John Brown, which said, in effect, that the price of repression is greater than the cost of freedom.
>
> The situation has changed in later years. It is not now a fight between advocates of the higher education and the industrial education, but it is a fight against an attempt to deliver the whole Negro race into the hands of one boss.
>
> Booker Washington, under two administrations, has been made the political dictator of the Negro race with the distribution of all patronage. This is not only unfair but illogical, since he has practically opposed Negro suffrage. Particularly it is undemocratic and is being used by the South and certain great vested interests to reduce the Negro to economic slavery.
>
> Against this the advanced wing of the American Negroes, as represented by the Niagara Movement, is making a determined fight. The vested interests who so largely support Mr. Washington's program of Negro docility and usefulness to others are, to a large extent, men who wish to raise in the South a body of black laboring men who can be used as clubs to keep white laborers from demanding too much.

30

The Over-Look

To form brave men educate boldly—*Richter*

GODFREY OF BOUILLON

A Talk to the Graduates of the Baltimore Colored High School.

Once upon a time near a thousand years ago a boy was born in the vine clad hills of lower Lorraine, on the borders of the great kingdom of France, and his name was called "The Peace of God." In a sense the greatest age of Europe was the Middle Age. And the greatest deeds in the Middle Age were certainly the Crusades. And the greatest of the Crusaders was this same boy, Godfrey Bouillon. He was a strong boy, square and sturdy, rich and nobly born. His mother, Ida, was of the greater grandchildren of mighty Charlemagne himself, and his father, Eustace of Boulogne, claimed for his for-bear Lohengrin, that mysterious knight of the Swan with whose music Wagner weds the world.

Now the century when the child Godfrey saw first the light that lingers in the valley of the Meuse, was a century curious in the annals of men. It was a day of wars and rumors of wars: a day when there seemed but two things for men to do: fight and pray—to be a soldier or a priest. And then when priests themselves began to bear arms Europe became one armed camp, bristling with unsheathed swords, with every man's hand ready to be raised against his brother, with governments built on blood and iron and last authority lying in the Strength of the Strong.

In all this day of turmoil and red murder, when mighty men were welding mighty nations, when the splendor of a hundred kings stood built upon the voiceless misery of the many, one bond alone, and that Religion, made out of Europe a commonwealth, with the Pope of Rome as king of kings. Only the Truce of God could bring momentary peace to the clash of ceaseless arms. In the deft hands of mighty Hildebrand, the lowly Italian boy who in 1073 became father of Christendom, the spiritual authority of the church began to be felt in the political affairs of men in every corner of Europe. He put down the mighty from their seats and exalted them of low degree, and men stricken suddenly with a sense of sin and seeing the completion of a thousand years of Christian history began to ask: Is not the end of this world near? Is not this the waning of that millenium wherein Evil was to be chained to Earth?

But the authority of the Church was not easily acknowledged by all the proud and half-barbaric giants who were building a new kingship, and among those who

From *The Horizon: A Journal of the Color Line* 6 (June 1910):1–5.

refused to bow to Hildebrand was Godfrey of Bouillon, soon to be Duke of Lower Lorraine, that wonderful smiling valley which lies between the Meuse, the Moselle and the storied Rhine.

When the great war burst between the fourth Henry, Emperor of the Holy Roman Empire and the Vicar of Christ at Rome, it was Godfrey of Bouillon, a beardless youth of twenty, strong as a bull, fearless and hotheaded, who flew to the forefront of the Emperor's armies and slew with his own hand that Swabian Rudolph whom the Pope had anointed King. The battle flickered and flamed until its curses filled the world and its blood flowed from Rhine to Tiber. The Pope brought the Emperor to his knees as pleading, penitent, in the snows of Conossa, and the Emperor in turn besieged the Pope in the very walls of the Holy city and the first warrior to leap through the breach was Godfrey of Bouillon.

And this was his Commencement. This was the day when halting and looking forward and back this man of twenty-five asked himself: "Whither am I going, where is the way?" To all men soon or late, comes the commencement of life. To some of these young friends of mine it comes tonight—to some its full questioning has not come, but it will come. Sometime, somewhere, each soul of you will pause and ask the Riddle of the World-old Sphinx: "Where and whither is the way?"

And because this man a thousand years ago faced this Commencement question so honestly and answered it with so much of error and yet with so sincere a striving for the right—for this reason I bring him back from out the gray forgotten ghosts of the mighty dead, and set him here amid this scene of youth and strength, of bounding life and endless hope; here to spark wisdom unto these young graduates with his dead lips.

Behold then, the year 1094—the place, the fairest valley of Europe, radiant with harvest and scarred with war, laughing with blue rivers, and shadowed by great yellow sunlit hills. The man is Godfrey of Bouillon, a giant of 36, the acknowledged Lord of all this wealth and power surrounded with the pomp and circumstance of a reigning monarch and yet gloomy, sick, dissatisfied with sin upon his soul.

Dissatisfied with all that deep unfathomed dissatisfaction of a man who finds the most glittering of the world's prizes turning to ashes in his hand. For what after all seemed his sordid destiny—to eat and drink and then to drink and eat again; to fight and quarrel with his own kinsmen and friends; to tax and oppress his own people in order to parade and show among them.

A thing that seemed to many the greatest thing on earth, seemed to him as he sat and mused, the smallest. So sometime it may seem to you: to dress in silk and fine linen, to spend money freely, to rule and order men, to fly in yachts and automobiles. "What more can a man want?" cry the foolish voices of the world, but the wise say with Godfrey of Bouillon: "more, much more." These are but the trappings of the world, not its substance: the glorious shadows but not the world itself.

So thought this ruler of men in 1094 as he watched the white road winding by the blue waters of the Meuse. On that road he saw as he sat the figure of a man. He was an old man, diminutive and in appearance almost contemptible. He wore a woolen shirt and over this a brown and girded mantle reaching to his knees, leaving his arms and legs and feet bare. It was Peter the Hermit: and Godfrey of Bouillon had known him as a boy in his father's house.

Today he listens to a prophet. For this wanderer, mean, curious and strange as he was in appearance was the anointed fore-runner of a great Idea. We do not have Ideas says one, they have us and force us in the Arena to fight for them. Just as in this city seventy-five years ago Benjamin Lundy forethought Emancipation, just as in Palestine John the Baptist foreshadowed the Christ, so in 1094 Peter the Hermit foreran that mighty movement called the Crusades, destined in the fulness of time and in ways he did not dream of, to unite Chistendom, to civilize Europe and to give birth to the Renaissance and modern intellectual and religious freedom.

As Peter the Hermit impressed Godfrey of Bouillon so he impressed all Europe until at the call of Pope Urban II an unnumbered multitude of men cried, "It is the Will of God." and started to rescue Jerusalem from the grasp of the Seljukian Turks.

I have not time to tell you of all the strangeness of that world movement; of how led by varied and meaner motives and yet continually overhung by the blaze of that great idea of personal sacrifice for the redemption of the Redeemer's Tomb, millions of men, women and children offered up their lives in willing sacrifice and died hoping to live again, as indeed they do live tonight in your memories and mine. Chiefly, I want to speak of Godrey of Bouillon; of the *deception and discouragement* that marked the beginning of his crusade; of how he *under-rated* and then *over-rated* the strength of his enemy, *quarrelled* with his friends and *hesitated* at his task; of how he let the Demon of *cruelty* and *hate* mar his greatest victory and yet how finally was crowned *Defender of the Sepulchre of Christ* and lies today buried on the mount of Crucifixion—all this I will tell you, not simply for its own interest but because in the Crusade which you and I are fighting for human freedom and the abolition of that last refuge of Barbarism—the Color line, you and I have met and will meet deception and discouragement, will under-rate and over-rate the forces against us, will stoop to cruelty and quarrel with each other and yet in His good time will triumph on the everlasting hills. It is the Will of God.

Blithe was the morning when in mid-July 1094 the splendid cortege of first Crusade moved down the Danube from Ratisbon with faces set South and eastward and with their war cry: "It is the Will of God." Behind lay famine and unrest, before lay the Tomb of Christ beleaguered by the infidel, along a way strewn with bones and superstition, blood and sin. Marvellous was the cavalcade that thus started for Jerusalem. To gather his army Godfrey all but sold his kingdom and looked with pride on 80,000 foot soldiers and ten thousand horsemen who followed in his train, while other armies followed other leaders from all the breadth of Europe. With Godfrey rode his two brothers Eustace and Baldwin, the Counts of Hainault, and of Grai, Durdon de Gontz whom Tasso afterward immortalized and a hundred other knights and noblemen whom the world remembers. They rode in flashing armor, with hawk on wrist and plume in helm; with banners fluttering on the breeze and high-born ladies riding with them, and on their shoulders blazed the crimson cross of the Crusader. Yet the cavalcade had little of solemnity. It was rather, like some great holiday procession, joyous, splendid, almost insolent in its bravado. Some in that vast throng rode for the glory of conquest and thirst of power: some rode for lust of body and lusts of gold: some rode to be riding, in restless quest of adventure, but before them all rode Godfrey of Bouillon, a man whom men of his own described, despite his bulk and power, as "tantum lenis"—so gentle, with "mira humilitas"—wonderous humility, and "modestia jam imitanda monachis"—almost the modesty of a priest. To start upon one's life work on a night like this well prepared, in pomp and circumstance and yet in gentleness, humility and modesty, this is *one* lesson of the first Crusade.

And then, began the trouble, the temptation and the danger.

Eastward when Europe steps into Asia across the shining Bosporus, sits a great city on a site perhaps the loveliest of earth. And here in Constantinople at the end of the 11th Century Alexius Commenus ruled the last remnants of a mighty empire and saw with dismay the approach of hundreds of thousands of Crusaders. He had, to be sure, invited their aid but he had looked for no such host as this and feared them. Against such masses he could not defend his borders and accomplish his selfish ends, by force, and so he used deception. He flattered and cajoled the simple giants, played on their mutual jealousies, indulged their baser passions, until honest men like Godfrey of Bouillon, sat mystified and bewildered saying: "This is our friend and yet I do not understand his plain dishonesty. Where lies the way to the Tomb of the Redeemer?" Just as you and I when we ask but the simple treatment of men and human beings are met with lying lips and flattering circumlocutions, with open honest faces which conceal dishonest thoughts and the Songs of that sort of Sunday School Christianity which builds itself on a parade of narrow heathenism.

Two weary months the Crusaders struggled with the deceit of Alexius but on the 1st of March 1097 they stepped at last on Asiatic soil and in June not less than six hundred thousand Crusaders crying: "It is the Will of God," flocked around the walls of the first of the fortresses that guarded the way to Jerusalem, the ancient city of Nicaea.

Now the first temptation of men who unflattered and uncajoled, turn with determination to face an enemy, is to despise that enemy; to think that a bad cause means necessarily bad defenders and that they who block the highways to Jerusalem are by that very token, knaves and cowards. Would this were so; would I were able to assure these men and women of tomorrow that only cowards defend the wrong, and that they run before the onslaught of the Righteous. It is not so. . . .

At last overwhelmed by numbers the city fell, but before it fell the Crusaders had learned one thing and that was to respect their opponents. And this respect grew gradually in the hearts of many to admiration and fear. They coveted the rich cities that they saw in the luxurious east. They began to criticize and to despise themselves and quarrel with each other. The suns of burning Phrygia beat upon their heads and sickness and disease decimated them. The children perished and women died in agony. Gaunt, hungry-eyed, horseless and weighted with their iron armor, the knights swarmed about the crumbling walls of Antioch, great Antioch, the wonderful. Daily deserters sneaked away and joined the infidels; the ravenous killed and ate human beings; and half-naked knights staggering back to Constantinople blasphemed and cried with Guy of Tarentum: "O God Omnipotent: where is thy Power? If thou art omnipotent, why dost thou let these things be done?"

For seven awful months they besieged Antioch and saw hundreds and thousands of their fellows fall. Yet Godrey of Bouillon stayed steadfast.

At last through treachery, the city fell and victory was worse than defeat. Murder, drunkenness and prostitution ran riot. The leaders quarrelled and fought and even Godfrey of Bouillon drew his sword to fight Behonmond of Tarentum over a silken tent. But the Ideal was not dead and the manhood of the Crusaders was not sapped. . . . They were as we too often are, dazzled and cast down by the apparent endless power of those who hate as we quarrel among ourselves, criticize our own motives blindly and sink to sin and degradation, forgetting the high crusade for human rights to which the Spirit of Jesus Christ as well as that of every true and pure prophet of humanity continually impels us. And when revivified and inspired we press forward again, the last great temptation of earnest human beings faces us, as it faced Godfrey and his Crusaders—the temptation of Hate—the temptation that identifies the deed hated with the person who does it—which burns the criminal and not the crime; which despises, not ignorance, but the unfortunates who are ignorant; which curses the infidel and not his faithlessness; which crucifies Sin and saves no Sinner. . . .

The deed was done. Jerusalem was delivered. The hosts of Crusaders turned joyously homeward laden with spoil. But behind them they left Godfrey of Bouillon, an uncrowned King who called himself Defender of the Sepulchre of Christ and who with but a handful of knights kept watch and ward about the burial place of the purest and greatest of the prophets of the Brotherhood of Man. Slowly and doubtfully Godfrey of Bouillon learned his life lesson. From a head-strong warrior eager to fight for fighting's sake, he became, in the awful tutelage of years, an humble, silent man, a law giver and father of his people, a protector of Christian and Pagan alike and a king who would not wear a crown of gold where his master had been crowned with thorns.

So in the fulness of time he triumphed, and in one little year from the day he was made Defender of Christ's Tomb, they buried his worn and lifeless body on Mount Calvary. . . .

Young men and women of the graduating class:

In all this human story that I bring, the lesson for you and for me is too obvious to need much comment. All life is a learning. So little have you already learned with your diligence that we call such occasions as these Commencements—the beginnings of more serious study. Of these lessons to be learned by you, some are the lessons of all living: Work, Recreation, Honesty, Temperance, Chastity and Sacrifice. But some are lessons peculiar to us who go upon this Last Crusade, the crusade to deliver from the Heathen the Sacred Truth of Human Equality and Brotherhood; to beat back the hateful heresy that the world and its joys and op-portunities belong to people of any one race or color; to lift high the banner which guides all humanity of every race and color; to the kingdoms of culture and courtesy and liberty—the rightful heritage of all men everywhere.

Not as doubtful burden, but as a badge of distinction let us wear the cross of this Crusade upon our shoulders crimson with the blood of our fathers. Remem-bering in our weary march the things which the first Crusade taught Godfrey of Bouillon:

1. Not to be bewildered by deception; to listen with all courtesy to those false voices within and without the race that counsel us to be satisfied and acquiescent under the intolerable oppression and insult that faces us everywhere: to listen with courtesy to such falsehoods and pay no manner of attention to them, remembering that the races who are content with slavery are slaves, the animals who are willing to cringe and follow are dogs, and the men who are satisfied are dead.

2. Let us learn neither to under-rate nor over-rate the forces of evil leagued against us. They are powerful but not all powerful. They are mighty but not almighty. To win the battle of human freedom today calls for every bit of nerve and muscle we can muster but it can be done and the greatest hindrance is not lack

of power but lack of knowledge; the monstrous assumption that present civilization with its hypocrisy, lying and stealing, its prostitution and poverty, its ignorance and cruelty is the last word of human possibility. To forget human betterment in such a wilderness is to forget God.

3. Let us not dream that the end of human striving is human hatred. The greater good of the Crusaders came not to Christians alone but to the Christian and Pagan both. The doctrine of White men up and Black men down is not to be successfully opposed by a doctrine of Black men up and White men down. In no selfish racial narrowness must this the last and mightiest of the crusades be conceived, but on a platform as wide as God's heaven and broad as his footstool, on which there is room for every creature, regardless of sex and color and birth, to strive untrammelled for the best that he is or may become.

To this high mark my brothers and sisters, let us lift our banners and march onward toward the ramparts of Jerusalem. It is the Will of God.

31

The Over-Look

But by my love and hope I conjure thee: throw not away the Hero in thy soul! Keep holy thy highest hope!

Nietzsche.

THE NATIONAL ASSOCIATION FOR THE ADVANCEMENT OF COLORED PEOPLE

On the one hundreth anniversary of Abraham Lincoln's birth there was issued in New York City a call to conference. This call was signed by Jane Addams, William Lloyd Garrison, Jenkin Lloyd Jones, Brand Whitlock, Charles Edward Russell, Mary W. Ovington, William English Walling and others. The manifesto said: "Is this not a fitting time for the Nation to comtemplate the condition of its Colored citizens?"

As a result of this call two conferences have been held in New York City: in May, 1909 and 1910. These conferences were earnest quiet talks with a few public meetings at which speakers of national prominence, expressed themselves in no uncertain terms.

The result was the formation of the *National Association for the Advancement of Colored People.*

The object of this organization is to arouse and organize public opinion among American citizens to the present unjust treatment of Colored citizens and to the danger of such treatment to the democratic and religious ideals of the land.

The methods of work employed by this organization will be simple and direct, and will consist in the main of:

a. Getting reliable information.

b. Placing such information at the disposal of the public.

c. Publishing tracts, pamphlets and a monthly periodical.

d. Maintaining a legal bureau in connection with the Constitution League.

e. Endeavoring to increase co-operation in the efforts of the Colored people and their friends in all directions.

f. Holding conferences and public meetings and maintaining a lecture bureau.

The Association is organized as follows: At its head stands an honorary committee of one hundred citizens. They are at present so far as selected:

NEW YORK CITY.

Miss Gertrude Barnum
*Rev. W. H. Brooks
*Prof. John Dewey
Mr. W.E.B. Du Bois

From *The Horizon: A Journal of the Color Line* 6 (July 1910): 1–5.

*Miss Maud R. Ingersoll
*Mr. Paul Kennaday
*Mrs. F. R. Keyser
*Dr. Charles Lenz
*Mr. Jacob W. Mack
*Mrs. M. B. MacLean
*Mr. John E. Milholland
Rev. Horace G. Miller
*Mrs. Max Morgenthau, Jr.
*Mr. James F. Morton, Jr.
Mr. Henry Moskowitz
Miss Leonora O'Reilly
Rev. A. Clayton Powell
Mr. Charles Edward Russell
*Mr. Jacob H. Schiff
*Prof. E.R.A. Seligman
Rabbi Joseph Silverman
Mrs. Anna Garlin Spencer
*Mrs. Oswald G. Villard
Miss Lillian D. Wald
*Mr. Wm. English Walling
*Bishop Alexander Walters
Dr. Stephen S. Wise
Rev. Jas. E. Haynes, D. D., Brooklyn
Rev. Jno. Haynes Holmes, Brooklyn
Miss M. R. Lyons, Brooklyn
Miss M. W. Ovington, Brooklyn
Dr. O. M. Waller, Brooklyn

NEW YORK AND NEW JERSEY.

Hon. Thos. M. Osborne, Auburn, N.Y.
Mr. W. L. Bulkley, Ridgefield Park, N.J.

MASSACHUSETTS.

Miss Maria Baldwin, Boston
Mr. Francis J. Garrison, Boston
Mr. Archibald H. Grimke, Boston
Mr. Albert E. Pillsbury, Boston
Mr. Moorfield Storey, Boston
Mr. Wm. Monroe Trotter, Boston
Dr. Horace Bumstead, Brookline

OHIO.

Prest. Charles T. Thwing, Cleveland
Mr. Chas. W. Chesnutt, Cleveland
Prof. W. S. Scarborough, Wilberforce

ILLINOIS.

Miss Jane Addams, Chicago
Mrs. Ida B. Wells Barnett, Chicago
Dr. C. E. Bentley, Chicago
Mrs. Celia Parker Woolley, Chicago

PENNSYLVANIA.

Dr. N.F. Mossell, Philadelphia
Dr. Wm. A. Sinclair, Philadelphia
Miss Susan Wharton, Philadelphia
Mr. R. R. Wright, Jr., Philadelphia

MARYLAND & THE DISTRICT OF COLUMBIA.

Rev. Harvey Johnson, D. D., Baltimore, Md.
Hon. Wm. S. Bennet, Washington, D.C.
Mr. L.M. Hershaw, Washington, D.C.
Justice Wendell P. Stafford, Washington, D.C.
Mrs. Mary Church Terrell, Washington, D.C.
Rev. J. Milton Waldron, Washington, D.C.

THE SOUTH.

Prest. John Hope, Atlanta, Ga.
Mr. Leslie Pinckney Hill, Manassas, Va.

Of these persons, those whose names are starred form an executive committee of fifteen. The officers of this association are as follows:

President of the General Committee, Hon. Moorfield Storey, of Boston.
Treasurer, John E. Milholland, Esq.
Assistant Treasurer, Mr. Oswald Garrison Villard.
Chairman of the Executive Committee, Mr. Wm. English Walling.

The Executive Officers are:

Director of Publicity and Research, Mr. W.E. B. Du Bois.
Executive Secretary, Miss Frances Blascoer.

The Association occupies a suite of offices at 20 Vesey Street, New York, in the building of the New York Evening Post.

In other words we have at last organized and started a business organization, housed in the metropolis of the nation and devoted to the solution of the Negro problem in accordance with the best ideas of modern philanthropy and democracy. Back of the organization stand men of thought, heart and wealth— all we need now is your help and co-operation.

HOW TO HELP THE N. A. A. C. P.

To help us, join us. Join our membership: that is the first thing to do. There are several grades of membership, varying in cost from one dollar for associate membership to three hundred dollars for life membership. Ordinary, full membership costs two dollars a year—a sum within the reach of all. Such members receive all notices and publications. If you are willing to join or want more information, write to Miss Frances Blascoer, 20 Vesey St., New York City. Clubs, churches and organizations may join us.

Besides this we shall organize many lines of individual and co-operative work. There are many persons, white and colored willing to give some time to this great cause if they knew something they could do and feel that it would be effective. If you are such a person, and want work, much or little, write me at 20 Vesey Street, New York. Now for a long, strong pull toward the great goal. Let us get to work.

ATLANTA UNIVERSITY

During the last twenty years Atlanta University has borne the brunt of the great fight for Negro freedom. She has maintained a standard of scholarship, kept high her ideal and single her purpose, and untempted by money has stood unswervingly for the Higher Education of Negro youth. Fifteen—even ten years ago, there was scarcely a voice in the land raised to defend the Negro college. Today no thinking man dares to deny its right to exist. The credit for this change of front lies in no small degree at the feet of Atlanta University.

Thirteen years ago I determined to go South and study the Negro problem. President Horace Bumstead invited me to Atlanta University and I accepted the call. For now more than a decade it has been my high privilege to work with the noble men and women and lovable students of this institution, where there is no color line. I count it a high honor to have labored in this great work. The institution has generously backed my efforts, even when these efforts cost friendships and perhaps money. Not once have the trustees sought to curtail my freedom of thought and speech. I thank them, for I have spoken in these years in no uncertain tones; and to allow a black man today to stand up and talk out for his rights is a privilege granted in few places in the United States.

When in the past overtures have been made to me to leave the work at Atlanta and go, at higher salary, to Hampton, to Tuskegee, to the Public Schools of Washington and elsewhere, it has invariably seemed to me that my duty lay at Atlanta.

Finally, however, came this call from the National Association for the Advancement of Colored People—a pioneer organization, an experiment, but an attempt to do bravely and courageously a work that must be done. I accepted the call and with deep regret resigned from Atlanta University. I need not say, however, that the work of this institution will ever stand near my heart.

COMPULSORY EDUCATION AND THE NEGRO

A Talk to White Georgia

The opposition to compulsory education in Georgia is very largely due to:
1. Its cost, on account of the large Negro population.
2. An unwillingness to extend its benefits to Negroes at any cost.
1. The idea of most white Georgians is that Negro education is today costing them a great deal. A moment's facing of the real facts will prove this untrue. The State school fund by the thirty-fifth annual report of the State Department of

Education was apparently $1,786,588.33 in 1906. The sources of this fund were approximately as follows:

Direct taxes on property	$1,000,000.00
Direct taxes on polls	275,000.00
Indirect taxes	290,855.71
Income from Endowments	220,732.62
Total	$1,786,588.33

Negroes paid 4 per cent of the direct taxes, and so far as I can ascertain, about 34 per cent of the poll taxes, which makes $137,500. The indirect taxes fall as largely on the Negroes as on whites; they buy liquor and fertilizers, go to shows, and people the prisons.

The Negroes are entitled also to their *pro rata* share of endowments, since these are not a burden on present tax payers but a social heritage from a past in which Negroes helped accumulate the wealth by which the State bought railway property. 48 per cent of the indirect taxes and the endowments ($511,588.33) is $245,562.40; adding this to the direct taxes we have a Negro school fund of $386,112.40.

There was however $882,745.42 raised by local taxation. It is difficult to estimate the Negroes' share of this for a large part is raised by the indirect taxation like the tax on the street railroads on which Negroes ride, tax on businesses where the Negro spends his money etc., as well as by direct taxation.

It would be a conservative estimate to say that at least one tenth of this sum fell on Negroes who own over 4 per cent of the property and contribute at least another 6 per cent in indirect taxes. This would add the sum of $88,274.54 to the fund above making a grand total of $474,386.94 for Negro schools raised for the most part by Negroes themselves and the remainder justly belonging to them as citizens and workers. To this sum no living white man in Georgia contributes a single cent, nor is any white person the poorer for its existence.

Of course the sum is much smaller than one could easily calculate if it were not assumed that the burden of direct taxes fell on the one paying the tax. This assumption is of course absurd: who pays the taxes on a rented house, the renter or the landlord? The renter of course: the landlord passes the money in, but the amount of the house rent is always adjusted to the tax. The renter is the real tax payer in that case. If this be true, then the Negroes' real share of the million dollar school fund is nearer a quarter of a million of dollars than the $40,000 assigned. But waiving this point and assuming the Negro school fund to be $474,386.94, what is spent on Negro schools?

The answer to this is not clear in the reports but can be approximated.

The amount expended on schools was as follows:

Country schools	$1,477,062.95.
Local systems	1,273,900.27
Total	$2,750,963.22

Of this sum $2,166,815.28 was paid teachers, out of which colored teachers got 19 per cent or $412,785.51. This leaves $584,147.74 which was expended for buildings, supplies, superintendence etc. What part of this should be charged to

Negroes? The report is silent but certain facts are clear: very little time of super-
intendence is given to Negro schools, and very few supplies are furnished; of the
amount spent on building for Negroes we may judge by these figures:

School Property owned by School Boards:

White	$3,040,224	90.96%
Colored	301,785	9.04%
	$3.342,009	100%

It is fair to assume therefore that not more than 10 per cent of the $584,147.74
was spent on Negroes which makes the total cost of their schools $471,200.28. We
have therefore:

Negro school fund	$474,386.94
Cost of Negro schools	471,200.28
	$3,186.66

It is not of course pretended that the above figures are absolutely correct: They
may vary by thousands or even tens of thousands; but this is certain: if we assign
to the Georgia Negro an even approximately just share of the money which he
actually pays to the public treasurer, and if out of that social income which is not
an individual tax on any white man, we grant to Negroes, as justly we must, their
pro rata share according to population, then it can be proven beyond a reasonable
doubt that the education of Black Georgia is not today costing white Georgia a
single cent.

This is not all. Wealth is a social product, and not an individual acquisition. At
present we allow certain men to be custodians of this social wealth, partly because
of the worth of their services in helping the community to accumulate it and partly
because of their wise use of their trust. But we never forget where wealth in the
last analysis belongs—i. e., to the community. We take it for taxes, we seize it when
grossly misused, we limit the amount and method of its disposal. Why? Because
WE own it. We, i. e. organized society created the wealth in unison and it was not
created by any one man or corporation. If this is true, then every worker in the
community has some claim on this common wealth. If the community is ignorant,
this wealth provides schools not as a matter of almsgiving but as a matter of vested
right to a reasonable share of the social income.

In this common wealth the black man has a share. His services are indispensable
to the common wealth and his share of the social product is just an equitable as
any white man's. Here is a millionaire. Who made his wealth? His own ability and
foresight aided by the labor and co-operation of the community in which he lives.
The community taxes him for schools. That is right. But by what right does the
white portion of the community assume the sole right to profit by the taxes and
leave the Negroes in ignorance? Did Negroes do anything toward the accumulating
of this wealth? How many of the great fortunes of Georgia today are not built
primarily on Negro toil?

I come therefore to the second part of the paper:

2. Negro schools ought to be supported by the taxes on all people. Compulsory
education ought to double the school facilities of all races in Georgia. Why?

Because the social burden of Negro ignorance is greater than any possible cost of schools. Ignorance is costly because it—

A. *Increases poverty.* Wealth is a social product. Ignorant workers are inefficient workers. Education increases efficiency.

B. *Increase Crime.* Ignorant communities are more liable to crime. Education tends to eliminate crime; all history proves this and the history of the Negro especially.

C. *Lowers Morality.* Ignorance invites aggression. It encourages the Thief and the Swindler, and its tempts and shields the licentious.

D. *Spreads Disease.* The white death rate of the South can never be successfully lowered as long as the Negro death rate is high. Disease is infectious. Ignorance is the mother of infection.

If now then rests upon us like a great pall this burden of crime, disease and immorality and if the very burden increases our poverty, can we afford to let ignorance remain at any cost?

But, say some, we are afraid to make the Negro intelligent: we prefer to keep him a dumb driven ox. In that case then:

A. Cease to complain of Negro Crime.

B. Cease to complain of inefficient Negro labor.

C. Cease to dread consumption and epidemics.

D. Cease to believe in Human Progress for most human beings are colored.

E. Cease to call yourselves followers of Jesus Christ.

———

The true friend is not he who holds up Flattery's mirror.
In which the face to thy conceit most pleasing hovers;
But he who kindly shows thee all thy vices, sirrah!
And helps thee mend ere an enemy discovers.

Oriental, translated by W. R. Alger.

Name Index